THE
1975

LOVE, SEX & CHOCOLATE

DAVID NOLAN

MUSIC
PRESS

Published by Music Press Books
an imprint of John Blake Publishing Ltd
3 Bramber Court, 2 Bramber Road,
London W14 9PB, England

www.johnblakebooks.co.uk

www.facebook.com/johnblakebooks ⬛
twitter.com/jblakebooks ⬛

First published in paperback in 2017

ISBN: 978 1 78606 259 8

British Library Cataloguing-in-Publication Data:

A catalogue record for this book is available from the British Library.

Design by www.envydesign.co.uk

Printed in Great Britain by CPI Group (UK) Ltd

1 3 5 7 9 10 8 6 4 2

© Text copyright David Nolan 2017

Papers used by John Blake Publishing are natural, recyclable products made from
wood grown in sustainable forests. The manufacturing processes conform to the
environmental regulations of the country of origin.

Every attempt has been made to contact the relevant copyright-holders,
but some were unobtainable. We would be grateful if the appropriate
people could contact us.

This book is dedicated to all the teachers who helped and encouraged me at school. I've listed their names below…

CONTENTS

ACKNOWLEDGEMENTS

Many thanks to those who helped with the book: Jack Bowers, Emily Brinnand, Owen Davies, Daniel Deighan, Peter Devine, Ben Hiard, Ben Taylor and Charlie Watts. Double thanks to both Bens for photos and flyers. Appreciation also to James Hodgkinson and Ciara Lloyd at John Blake/Music Press Books.

FINGERS CROSSED: SOUND CONTROL, MANCHESTER, 5 DECEMBER 2012

The backstage rider that had been requested – particularly for a band few people had heard of – was as specific as it was entertainingly eccentric. It seemed to sum them up, in fact.

In the dressing room of the 150-capacity downstairs room of Sound Control in Manchester, the modest venue tucked away in the shadow of Oxford Road train station, the headline act had asked for something that had caught the eye of the people working there. Alongside the usual requests for alcohol (premium lager, please), towels (clean and dry) and food (pitta bread, hummus, salami and cheese – specifically, Emmental) was something slightly out of the ordinary.

'Six National Lottery scratchcards.'

'Really?'

'Yup.'

'OK, then. Why not?'

The band played a sold-out show that night – a full-on, crowd-surfing, a-ton-of-girls-at-the-front sold-out show that would later be seen as a turning point in their career. They didn't know it yet, but after this show they would barely go home for two years; they'd have two No. 1 albums – one in the US – and they'd chart a path through the many and varied venues of Manchester that would see them play the city's Arena almost exactly four years later.

That was all to come. For now, we are still at Sound Control in December 2012... and the band have just come offstage.

This was the first sold-out show they'd ever played – ordinarily they would have counted a fifty-strong crowd as a major achievement. To mark the success of the show, the promoters gave them a bottle of champagne to celebrate with. When it arrived in the dressing room, along with a set of appropriate glasses with which to drink it, the band chucked the glasses to one side and necked the champers from the bottle.

It was that kind of night.

But the reality was that, after deductions for catering – and scratchcards – the band came away from the gig that night with just a few pounds each.

But right now, draining the last of the free champagne backstage at Sound Control, that didn't matter. Because... there was always the scratchcards. And as the presence of the cards showed, here was a band that had hope on their side. Hope, even when the odds weren't necessarily in your favour. Hope, when in fact the odds were well and truly stacked against you.

Because… who knows? With a little luck – fingers crossed – things could go their way. *Couldn't they?* And if they didn't, there was always the chance of winning a few quid on the side.

Clever.

In the end, the scratchcards wouldn't be required. A telling mix of guitars, electronic pulses, big drums, a magpie-like habit of picking up the shiniest of influences, and an eye-catching yet vulnerable frontman would see them through to stadium status within a few short years.

The band had only settled on a name earlier that year, after trying out and dispensing with a variety of monikers that didn't quite suit them. The right name for a band is very important. Look at one of the support acts at the Sound Control gig – Catfish and the Bottlemen. They're not going to get very far with a name like that.

Despite a sound that showed more than a passing interest in the brash and bold stylings of the mid-1980s, the headliners had opted for a name that represented the previous decade: The 1975.

And they were about to well and truly hit the jackpot.

ONE

THE GOLDEN TRIANGLE

When singer Matthew Healy introduces himself and his band to audiences in Britain and around the world, he usually states, 'We're The 1975… and we're from Manchester.'

That's because The 1975 – like many bands before them – use the city of Manchester in the northwest of England as a flag of convenience. It's usually just easier to say 'Manchester' – people get it, straight away. Because of the city's musical history, it's like a kitemark of quality that immediately attracts interest and attention.

In reality though, bands that claim to be from Manchester will actually be from one of the many satellite towns and metropolitan boroughs that dot the conurbation of Greater Manchester and its surrounding counties: The Verve (Wigan), The Stone Roses (Trafford), Happy Mondays (the adjoining city of Salford). They're all considered 'Manchester' bands – just like The 1975.

But with the benefit that comes from being associated with the city that brought us Buzzcocks, Joy Division, Factory Records, The Haçienda nightclub and Oasis comes a potential deadweight of expectation. A look, a style, a sound and even an attitude is taken as a given if you arrive with the label of being a 'Manchester band'.

'I think the music industry wants us to be more from Manchester than we actually are,' Healy once explained to US radio station KDGE in the band's early days. 'There's quite a tribalist attitude to music in Manchester. There's an almost stoic adherence to past genres and bands. We've never really worn the Manchester badge of honour. We'd rather just make our own little world and work in that. There's a lot of relevant music coming out of Manchester but we are not a "Manchester band" at all. A geographical location is not a very inspiring thing to us.'

So… a band that happily introduces itself onstage as being from Manchester, yet firmly but gently dissociates itself with the city's hefty musical history. This is the first of many contradictions that will be a regular occurrence when laying out the story of Matthew Healy and the band he has led to world prominence: The 1975.

Despite the way Healy introduces his band, the geographical origins of The 1975 are tangled. The area that actually forms the main backdrop to their story isn't in Manchester at all; it isn't even in the wider area of Greater Manchester: it's Wilmslow in neighbouring Cheshire.

Stretching from its eastern border with Manchester across to Merseyside in the west, it's a semi-rural sprawl of towns and villages that hasn't made a huge dent on the nation's rock 'n' roll psyche. That's because Cheshire's musical connections are patchy, to say the least – but when they've happened, they've been occasionally notable: Joy Division's Ian Curtis grew up in Hurdsfield near Macclesfield; Joy Division drummer Stephen Morris is also a Macc lad, as were nineties indie band Marion. Tim Burgess of The Charlatans spent much of his childhood in Northwich. Noddy Holder of Slade lives in Prestbury. Doves – best known for their noughties hits 'There Goes The Fear' and 'Black and White Town' – all went to Wilmslow High School, the same school that would bring together members of The 1975.

Doves' lead singer Jimi Goodwin says 'Black and White Town' is a song he wrote specifically about Wilmslow life. 'Wilmslow is a town full of contradictions,' he told the *Macclesfield Express*. 'On the one hand you've got the middle-class nouveau riche – footballer, stockbroker, moneyed villain – but also a lot of less-moneyed people. I had friends from both sides and we all hated it. The hypocrisy of the place. I don't know, is it any different from anywhere in small-town England? As a kid I think it's normal to be frustrated and resent where you're from. That's what the song "Black and White Town" is about. It's something to kick against.'

Tucked just east of Manchester Airport, Wilmslow forms part of a triumvirate of well-heeled Cheshire towns that are noted for their gravel-drive affluence. So much so in fact, the area has generated its own nickname: 'Wilmslow forms part of the Golden Triangle,' says experienced Wilmslow-watcher Peter Devine of the *Wilmslow Guardian*. 'There's Wilmslow, Alderley Edge and Prestbury. It's an area of wealth. There are lots and lots of football players and football managers who tend to inhabit the area.'

'It's quiet,' Owen Davies told me. Owen is the former guitarist with Drive Like I Do, one of the many names The 1975 went under before success came their way. 'The Wilmslow/Alderley area is a little bit pretentious overall, but not necessarily in a bad way. Everyone knows everyone, people are friendly everywhere you go. I like the place. It's got that aura to it, but day in, day out, you don't pay any attention to that "Golden Triangle" thing. It's just any old town as far as we're concerned.'

But make no mistake: Wilmslow is moneyed. The people are largely suntanned of skin, whitened of teeth and highlighted of hair. It's where players from Manchester's two main football teams gravitate to – just a brisk forty-minute drive from both United and City's grounds. It's not a place you'd spot people dressed or acting outlandishly – it's posh, but in a rather Cheshire sort of way. In an uncharacteristically rude aside, Healy once described it to *Paper* magazine as, 'a bullshit nothing town near Manchester with no real counterculture.'

Peter Devine is a little kinder: 'It's got a real community feel but at the same time it can be a bit "us and them",' he explained. 'There's the nouveau riche that live here, but there's also the older rich who live on the outskirts. So you've got two distinct groups of people. Everything is understated here. The only people who flaunt their wealth are the nouveau riche. People who have lived here a long time – the old money – they don't flaunt it. If you walk down the high street there are watches in the windows for thousands of pounds – but it's still understated... though everything in that window is beyond the means of the average person. The wealth is understated. That's the essence of the place.'

The 1975 have never claimed that they had to drag themselves up by their bootstraps. Personally and musically, they've always been a bit more Blur than Oasis. But being slightly removed from Manchester meant they were able to do their own thing, in their own way, at their own speed. 'Living in that area [Wilmslow]... a lot of bands kind of embrace financial depravation, somewhere to get out of,' Healy would later explain to journalist Nic Harcourt. 'We were living in a very middle-class and suburban area. It meant that we kind of bubbled along for a long time. We couldn't resent where we were from. We didn't have loads of money, we didn't have "no" money – that kind of middle ground. Searching for your identity is very apparent in places that don't really have an identity.'

Like many of the places that hover on the outskirts of Manchester, Wilmslow has no music scene of its own. There are no venues as such. A young band might get a gig in near-by Macclesfield, but they'd have to head to Manchester to make any kind of headway. 'We kinda started out of boredom,' Healy would later explain when discussing how his adopted hometown inadvertently influenced his decision to start a band. 'There was no real scene in our town at that time and we were all looking for some way of expressing ourselves, I suppose.'

'Wilmslow hasn't really been regarded as a place of music,' continues Peter Devine. 'Maybe it passed Wilmslow by. Wilmslow is conservative. The majority of youngsters don't necessarily make their breakthrough in Wilmslow. It's more likely to be Manchester. Wilmslow is a place where people who have made wealth live rather than a place where you create music. When you've made your money out of music, you come here to retire.'

Retirement isn't on the cards for The 1975 for quite some time. A potent mix of indie-boy guitars, unashamed eighties funk, ambient electronica and an endlessly watchable and quotable frontman has seen the band rise from pubs to stadia in what might seem to some like an indecently short amount of time. But the reality is very different. The band's success has been built on nearly a decade of work. *Very hard* work. Manchester DJ Dan Deighan, who has watched the band from their very early days, offers this by way of example: 'Matthew's dad once said to me: "Don't get this wrong, they are the hardest-working group of lads you'll ever meet in your entire life. They've grafted for it. They're perfectionists."'

Healy's dad is actor Tim Healy, best known for his roles in the classic eighties British comic drama *Auf Wiedersehen, Pet* and, more recently, the ITV sitcom *Benidorm*. His mum is actress, *Loose Women* TV presenter and tabloid favourite Denise Welch. Healy junior's upbringing is another aspect of the band's story that marks them out as being just that little bit different. Far from his 'showbiz' background helping him along the way, Matthew Healy has managed to find success on his own terms, nimbly avoiding the negative tag of 'showbiz kid' and moving past it.

'In the early years of growing up, you're living in a creative environment,' he told the *Guardian* in 2014. 'But you've got to remember, my parents weren't embraced by the mainstream till I was seventeen – *Loose Women* and all that. I was already in a punk band. So when you grow up in that environment, there's a weird thing of not wanting to be like your parents because you're an individual. But also being brought up in an environment where expressing yourself is endorsed. It's all right. Creativity is a facility of the human brain, but if you're brought up in an environment where it's OK to express yourself then that's going to translate into the type of person you are.'

Despite the Manchester/Cheshire conundrum, Matthew Healy was actually born in Barnet, North London on 9 April 1989. While he was still a baby, the family moved to High Mickley in Northumberland. At the time, his Newcastle-born dad Tim had been appearing in two high-profile TV shows at the same time: BBC's *Casualty* and ITV's *Boon*. His mum Denise, also from the northeast of England – Tynemouth – was at that point mainly a stage actress. She'd have her first taste of fame in the early nineties in the ITV military drama series *Soldier Soldier*.

Music was a major part of the Healy household. 'My mum was big into Motown, like Martha Reeves and the Vandellas, Kim Weston and stuff like that,' Matthew would later tell the *Some Kind of Awesome* website. 'While my dad was massively into the Stones, Wilson Pickett, Otis Redding, so that all played a part.'

Thanks to his northeast connections – and the fact that he's a highly accomplished singer – Tim Healy could boast a host of rock 'n' roll friendships, and Matthew would later claim he learned to play guitar on an instrument used on Dire Straits' *Brothers In Arms* album. 'He expected me to be a rock star,' Healy junior would later say of his dad. 'Mark Knopfler [Dire Straits] and Brian Johnson [AC/DC] would occasionally come around, so rock stars walked among us.'

Despite Tim Healy's musical track record, it's Matthew's mum Denise who can claim to have had the family's first hit single. In 1995 she got to No. 23 in the charts with her double-A side 'You Don't Have To Say You Love Me/Cry Me A River', after she was featured singing during an episode of *Soldier Soldier*. Young Matthew appeared briefly in the video for the song – not the last time he'd show a face in one of his mum's productions. Despite her success, Welch is typically self-deprecating about her singing skills: 'As an actor we all do bits and pieces of singing, but I'm really not very good,' she later told the *Macclesfield Express*. 'Tim is the singer out of the pair of us.'

She'd initially been offered a record deal by Simon Cowell after he'd had huge success with her co-stars Robson and Jerome. Cowell was generating hit after hit with his formula of turning TV stars into pop stars, even managing to create a hit for the Power Rangers. Welch's single was eventually released on Virgin and produced by the man behind The Wombles, Mike Batt. She would later recall hearing the song played on the Radio 1 Chart Show as she took young Matthew to his sixth birthday party.

Welch would also later write movingly about the post-natal depression that blighted her life after her son was born – as well as detailing her battles with drink and drugs. 'When I was about seventeen and my mum still drank, and we were at the house and we'd all had a drink and started talking about stuff,' Matthew once confessed to *Q* magazine, 'she got really, really upset and she said to me, "Do you know that when you were one and a half, for two months I would come into your room every night and lie down on the floor while you were asleep and try and love you?" Now, the reason why that resonated with me so much was because me and my mum are so close – we say, "I love you" in every phone call because we know that there's a chance it could go… It gets me a bit worked up.'

As a young child, Matthew would follow the itinerant

actors' lives of his parents, wherever that might lead. When his dad went to film a TV series in Australia, baby Matthew and his mum flew over several times to see him in the space of just a few months. Meanwhile, his mum landed parts in *Spender* with another actor turned singer, Jimmy Nail. She also appeared in kids' show *Byker Grove* alongside a young Ant and Dec, before she got her breakout role in *Soldier Soldier*, which meant filming in Cyprus.

But when Welch landed a part in Britain's most famous TV show – *Coronation Street* – the family moved to Wilmslow in Cheshire, an easy commute down the M56 to the studios of Granada TV in the centre of Manchester, where the long-running soap was filmed at the time.

Despite his parents' fame – and in Welch's case, her notoriety – Matthew Healy has always seemed to politely bristle at the suggestion that growing up in such a household has given him some sort of advantage: 'Maybe your sense of identity is slightly amplified because of the media, but because I've lived with the media I don't care about it,' he would later explain to Irish journalist Shelley Marsden. 'I know what it provides; all it's done is inspired me to be more my own person. Growing up, they were just jobbing actors. I used to spend my time backstage at theatres and in green rooms at the BBC. I'm not the son of Angelina Jolie, you know!'

Matthew was enrolled as a pupil at Lady Barn House in nearby Cheadle, an independent primary school. Jack Bower was a pupil at the time and remembers the school – and young Matthew Healy – well. 'It's a private school right next to Bruntwood Park – it's a beautiful school,' Bower told me. 'A few famous people sent their children there. When I was there, Jack and Chloe Madeley [the children of TV presenters Richard Madeley and Judy Finnigan] were at the school. It was a nice school with nice families – there were scholarships too, so there was a real mix of people. I was there from Year Three until Year Six. I remember Matthew in the playground. He was quite quiet.'

Bower remembers that Healy's parents' fame marked him out slightly from the other children at the school: 'At the time people would point out who his mum and dad were. We were quite aware – I think he was aware, too – that his mum and dad weren't a "normal" mum and dad. He was a bit different. We'd watch *Auf Wiedersehen, Pet* on Sky and my dad would say, "Oh that's Matthew's dad." We'd look out for his mum or dad at home time, to see if they were picking him up. But I think he was often picked up by a nanny, you didn't really see his mum and dad much at the school. But lots of kids at the school were picked up by nannies.'

Healy has had nothing but praise for his parents and his upbringing, particularly in the sense of it being a free and creative environment. 'My dad once said to me, "You be whatever you want to be, son",' he later explained to journalist Nick Duerden. '"You can be fucking John Lennon." When you hear that as a kid, the concept immediately becomes real.'

Around this time, Matthew had what would be a pivotal

musical experience – his first major live show. And it was a pretty major one: 'Michael Jackson – *HIS*tory Tour, 1996,' he later told the *Blahblahblahscience* music website. 'I was at that show in Wembley. I would have been about seven years old. It was one of the most memorable and important experiences I think I've ever had. Seeing him perform catalysed a real drive within me from an early age.'

Seeing Jackson also sealed a sense that Healy – to paraphrase Jackson himself – *wasn't like other guys*; seeing a figure as dramatic and seemingly different as the King of Pop go about his work was something that he could see himself doing: 'I remember once, I was sat in front of the TV and my dad's mates are all welders,' he recalled in an interview with *Gigwise*. 'They were sat behind me watching a video of Michael Jackson. And they were expressing their opinions about how alien he was, how unrelatable he was. And I remember thinking to myself, Well, I'm a lot more like him than I am like you.'

As his parents' careers flourished – mum Denise was by now a household name thanks to her role as Natalie Horrocks in *Coronation Street* – Matthew moved to King's School in Macclesfield, an independent day school that can trace its origins back 500 years. Matthew's interest in music was really flourishing at this stage and the youngster was to get his first taste of musical recognition – and his first write-up in the press – thanks to a charity song contest at the school. He won the contest by singing cover versions of 'There She Goes' by The La's and 'Don't Look Back In Anger' by Oasis.

Referencing the popular noughties TV talent show, the school's local paper, the *Macclesfield Express*, covered the win under the headline: 'Forget Will, Thank You But Goodnight Gareth – *Pop Idol* Has a New Heart Throb – Matthew Healy'. Despite the references to the then wildly popular *Pop Idol* TV show, Matthew was keen to explain to the paper that his musical tastes were a touch more exotic than the likes of Will Young and Gareth Gates. 'I love bands like Green Day and Blink-182,' he said. 'But I also love it when my dad plays Otis Redding and other singers from the sixties and seventies.'

Tellingly, Matthew let slip his future plans: 'I'd like to be a pop singer, but I really am just concentrating on my school work for now.'

That said, he would also taste a little of the attention his parents received as performers when, at the age of eleven, he appeared as an extra in *Coronation Street*. What's more, the episode – made to mark the fortieth anniversary of the show – was broadcast live. It would have given the youngster an idea of the buzz that is only available to those involved in live performance. Mum Denise was pregnant at the time the episode was broadcast – and Matthew's brother Louis was born soon after.

As well as these whiffs of what it would be like to be a performer, a heady, bizarre mix of music and visuals would start to swirl around young Healy in the late nineties and early noughties – all of which can now be spotted in his band's music to a greater or lesser degree. The previous decade had been represented by Jackson, art-school crossover artists like Peter Gabriel, the big drums and mainstream appeal of Phil Collins, the lo-fi blips and beeps of Yazoo and the synth-rock soundtracks of John Hughes' movies. 'John Hughes is cited as our No. 1 influence – *Pretty in Pink*, *The Breakfast Club*, *Weird Science*,' he later explained to *Stereoboard*. The filmic influence of Hughes' teen-orientated tales of eighties misfits would come to a head when The 1975 came to make their debut album: 'When we realised we were actually going to record all of these songs that we'd collected over years and years into an album, we thought, *Well, the way it needs to sound is as if John Hughes directed a movie about our lives and we were doing the soundtrack.*'

Hughes' films perfectly captured the teen angst of eighties teens with their boy meets girl – or occasionally, boy creates girl – storylines, garish fashions and strange splicing of UK and US synth-pop and rock on the accompanying soundtracks. The bands featured on some of Hughes' most famous films can all be heard in The 1975's music: INXS, Orchestral Manoeuvres in the Dark (OMD), and New Order (1982's *Pretty in Pink*); Kajagoogoo, Spandau Ballet, David Bowie (1984's *Sixteen Candles*) and Killing Joke, Kim Wilde, and OMD again in 1985's *Weird Science*.

Nineties R&B was in the mix too – everything from D'Angelo (a favourite of Denise Welch) to Eternal and Backstreet Boys. Then there was the all-embracing hugeness of Iceland's Sigur Rós and their precursor, the ambient soundscapes of Brian

Eno. 'I suppose it was Sigur Rós who first really blew me away,' Healy later told *Blahblahblahscience*. 'I remember hearing their first album and then totally emerging myself in all things Eno. Ambient music really speaks to me. I think it's because I first fell in love with music through film at a very early age – John Hughes' movies etc. Ambient music, at its best, commands you how to feel without the use of words – I think that's really powerful. More powerful, in fact.'

Then there were frontmen to study – the guy out front throwing shapes, walking the walk and talking the talk: the king of loose-limbed swagger, Mick Jagger; the take-your-top-off wildness of Iggy Pop; and the in-your-face intensity of Glassjaw's Daryl Palumbo. 'Glassjaw were one of the first bands I became really, really obsessed with in a heavy way,' Healy later told *Louder Than War*. 'They did heavy music that I really related too, I don't like heavy music that's a bit weak; it has to be heavy music as a representation of insanity.'

Then there were lyricists, The Streets 2002 release *Original Pirate Material* being a particular reference point: 'Probably one of the most important albums for us, partially due to our love of UK garage, although you may not be able to hear any of it in our records,' he later explained to journalist Katie Claire. 'When I moved to Manchester, UK garage was going on – we lived by a bar which was one of the UK garage bars. There were DJs on all the time, playing music that was so melodic, loads of syncopation; there was the Artful Dodger, Sweet Female Attitude – I became obsessed by it and it stayed with me. When

Original Pirate Material came out it was that music I loved – with poems. Here was a poet from where I came, he was at street level, he said it himself – *at street level*. I don't think there is a day that goes past I don't think about that sentence.'

The aggressive yet melodic end of punk represented by Daryl Palumbo was very much on Healy's horizon when Matthew went to see his favourite exponents of the genre, Green Day, at the Newcastle Arena. During this show he experienced a life-changing moment whereby he discovered first-hand what it was like to stand on a stage with thousands of pairs of eyes trained on you. And he discovered that he liked it. *A lot.* 'I was a tiny little kid, and this roadie threw me onto the stage,' he later remembered in an interview with *Q* magazine. 'They taught me the bassline and then I turned around and it was like, 10,000 people... Afterwards Billie Joe [Armstrong – Green Day's singer] comes and gives me a big hug and kisses me on the head and then I ran back down into the crowd to see my mates. And I think that the attention I had around me after that was the only thing I could focus on. Everyone wanted to congratulate me or back-pat me. And I signed an autograph – for a girl, a young girl who'd just seen me play. And I just thought at the time: This feels right, this feels appropriate. *I like this.*'

TWO

WILL YOU
SHUT UP!

Had it not been for a flying piece of school stationery, then Matthew Healy might not have left the King's School, he wouldn't have moved to Wilmslow High and he wouldn't have met the other members of The 1975.

Despite his success in the school talent show – and the glowing way teachers seemed to speak of him – Healy has since said that he was actually unhappy at King's. In fact, he has since said he hated it – and admits his behaviour at the school left something to be desired. Recalling his talent show win to the *Manchester Evening News* just before The 1975's success kicked in, Matthew explained: 'The ironic thing is that I got kicked out of that school shortly after [the talent show], it was a private school and I just wasn't interested in it. I was a bit naughty as a kid.'

One incident in particular led to Healy being 'kicked out' – in his words – of the prestigious establishment: 'I threw a protractor at somebody, and it got them between the eyes,' he told the *Some Kind of Awesome* website in 2013. 'It wasn't really as violent as it sounds. I also kind of really resented the whole thing because it was so silly. I thought the whole thing was a farce. Not school. But the school I was at. King's School in Macclesfield, there you go. I hate it.'

In the interest of fairness, I contacted King's to check this and other aspects of Healy's time there. They very politely confirmed that he had indeed been a pupil at the school and that he most certainly had won the talent competition... but they had no record of him being asked to leave the school and were very surprised to learn that Healy claimed he'd been 'kicked out'.

Either way, Healy then went to Wilmslow High School, a state school with an extremely good reputation thanks to its catchment area of towns in and around the 'Golden Triangle' – Wilmslow, Alderley Edge and Handforth: 'The school seems to attract really talented people,' says Peter Devine of the *Wilmslow Guardian*. 'Talented mathematicians, talented artists, footballers, tennis players, golfers – the list is endless. Perhaps that's partly due to the fact that maybe parents have a "can do" attitude down here. But many of them are wealthy and many can afford to buy instruments, say, that will allow them to succeed. It's a very inclusive school but it really brings people's talents to the fore.'

Despite being a good school in a well-heeled area, because it was a state school Wilmslow High was actually looked down on by some of the other Cheshire-set schools: 'I played a lot of sports there and we played against a lot of grammar schools,' says former pupil Owen Davies. 'They used to think we weren't as good because we were a comprehensive. I think it's a great school. That's down to the teachers and down to the people that went there. I loved it – genuinely all my close friends are still from Wilmslow High. I went through university, but I don't have many friends from there as I kinda stayed with the Wilmslow lot.'

For Matthew Healy – Matty to his friends – the new school didn't seem to have much effect on his larger-than-life personality, but he had an unusual way of avoiding fights. 'I used to bring sexuality to fighting at school,' he told *Rolling Stone*. 'If a kid was trying to fight me, I'd call boys, like, "Baby", and tell them, "I want to suck your dick" or something. You know, like, I'd throw them off.'

As he entered his teens Healy's interest in punk – not to mention that formative experience onstage with Green Day – had led him to want to form a band. He found four other like-minded souls at Wilmslow High. Future The 1975 drummer George Daniel had come to Wilmslow via Brussels and Seattle; guitarist Adam Hann came into the school from Handforth and bass player Ross MacDonald came from nearby Macclesfield. Guitarist Owen Davies – whose family had moved to Wilmslow from Leicester when he was a baby – was also with them from day one and was a vital witness to the earliest days of the band that would become The 1975. The original five would eventually become just four – for that we can blame a very well-known Manchester football team…

All five lived a few miles apart but it appears that it's Healy and Daniel who have a particular bond: 'You've got to remember,' Healy would tell *FaceCulture* website in 2013, 'that with me and George – with all the boys, but especially [George] – there's only been about a week, spread out over ten years that we haven't seen each other every day.'

He explained why: 'Our musical and stylistic and emotional vocabulary is very much one and the same. Most people start a band when they're sixteen or seventeen when they've decided, Oh, alternative music, that's what I'm about, that's the kind of kid I am. We started a band when we were thirteen – before you've even decided it. So we've always had this purity of creating music because we love music and the way it works and the way it makes you feel, not because of how many haircuts or leather jackets you have… nowadays we're a bit like that! We didn't actively search for an aesthetic. We just know. We're like an extension of each other.'

George Daniel, meanwhile, had a far more down-to-earth reason for wanting to be in a band – if you had a band rehearsal you could legitimately skip lessons, simple as that.

That said, Daniel, Healy, Dann and MacDonald were all musically-minded; by his own admission, Owen Davies was the odd one out: 'The other guys all went down the music route at school. I didn't even take music at school as a subject until later on, at A-levels. I wouldn't say I was from a musical background or had musical interests from the off. I remember when I was either fourteen or fifteen my dad got me a guitar for Christmas. And I remember looking at him thinking, what the hell is this? What am I going to do with this? I started having lessons and getting into it.

'Also, at that age, you're finding yourself and the music you're listening to kinda defines you. I was very much the mosher, chin pierced, nose pierced, all that. You get into going to gigs and stuff and one thing led to another. I was a bit weird, to be honest with you. I was kind of on the fence, because I did a lot of sport which a lot of the moshers just wouldn't do. Whereas I did both, which was a bit weird, I guess.'

Adam Hann started playing guitar relatively late – but soon made up for it with a dedication that bordered on the obsessive: 'I was around fifteen or sixteen,' he explained to journalist Tzvi Gluckin. 'My cousin played – he came to visit and brought his guitar and a little practice amp. The next day I went to the local music shop and bought a 10-watt Marshall amp and an Epiphone SG [guitar]. I had lessons for a bit, but I was obsessed so I'm mainly self-taught. I would do really monotonous things – parts I was trying to learn – to a metronome. I would play it slow and then speed it up and up until I could play it at the correct tempo. I used to spend hours sitting in my room doing things like that.'

Owen Davies: 'I remember when Adam had never played a

guitar in his life and got his first one. He'd come round to mine a few times and me and Adam would jam. We didn't really know each other that well at the time. I knew Ross very well. I used to play football with him in the clubs when I was younger, so we'd known each other since I was seven, six.'

The Healys had moved to the even leafier area of Lindow between Alderley Edge and Wilmslow by this stage. As it happens, Peter Hook of Joy Division and New Order was a neighbour and he remembers the teenage Matthew Healy: 'He's actually a neighbour of mine,' Hook told *Gigwise* in 2014. 'I know his mother very well. He came up to me when I was judging a competition with Denise and I met him. God, he must have been thirteen, fourteen, and he told me that he loved Joy Division and he was forming a band.'

George Daniel would later recall the first time he met Healy and the others in an interview with the BBC: 'I was just kicking around the music department at our high school. We knew of each other but we weren't really friendly. We just knew of each other's faces from playing in school bands.'

Adam Hann is cited as being the chief instigator in bringing the band together, specifically to play at a charity youth event called Macclesfield Youth Bands. 'I knew of Matty and Ross because my girlfriend at the time was in their form at school,' Hann explained in an interview with Radio 1. 'So I got her to ask them if they wanted to play some covers at this gig.'

Guitarist Owen Davies: 'We just had this idea, why don't we do a gig? At the time I think it was just supposed to be one gig for Macclesfield Youth Bands. It was at Macclesfield Senior Citizens' Hall and I think it was a charity event. We just thought, *Let's do a gig and see what happens*. So Adam got hold of me, Matty and Ross. Matty was singing on the drums to start with. We did a few rehearsals with Matty singing on the drums. We quickly realised we didn't want to do it like that.'

Singing and playing drums simultaneously is difficult at the best of times and not the best way of putting on much of a show at a gig. Ross MacDonald suggested drafting in George Daniel, two years below them. After initial concerns that the extremely tall yet fresh-faced Daniel was too 'odd' and 'looked about nine', the drummer was asked to join in to free up Healy as singer.

As the youth club gig approached, they knocked together a set of cover versions: songs by US punk band Me First and The Gimme Gimmes, Lit, Velvet Revolver, Bon Jovi and even the theme from eighties movie *Ghostbusters* by Ray Parker Jnr. 'Some woman called Sheila started this run of gigs for underage kids,' Healy later recalled to journalist Jason Karaban. 'I think she was like a hippy council worker – and they [the gigs] soon turned into a riot. We would go and play there, doing covers of punk songs and *Ghostbusters*. It was so drunken and personal. After doing that for a while we wrote a song and thought, *Let's just do this. This is well better than going to school or work.*'

The band had to decide on a name – they went with the distinctly emo-ish You And Me Versus Them. It would be the first of many, many names they went under.

'I remember it was a strange sensation,' original guitarist Owen Davies told me. 'I'd never been on a stage before and the gig went down well. It was great. The organisers were really good; there was probably about 200 people there for the first night. We had a great response, we did a lot of covers. I can remember it quite well actually. We did the *Ghostbusters* theme tune, which we thought was a great idea at the time, "Livin' on a Prayer" by Bon Jovi. We did Velvet Revolver's "Slither", "My Own Worst Enemy" by Lit. A couple of other songs as well. We *loved* it though. I remember throwing my plectrum into the crowd, thinking I was some sort of superstar. Then twenty minutes after the gig I found it again, there on the floor, which I found quite funny.'

The band played a series of gigs for Macclesfield Youth Bands and the charity nights alternated between Macclesfield's Senior Citizens Hall and the Festival Hall in Alderley Edge. Perhaps starved of entertainment, local kids latched onto the band almost immediately: 'We went down really well as soon as we started playing,' Owen Davies told me. 'We had a mini cult following, I'd say a few people would go to every gig. And everywhere we played we'd get a good reception – that's why we wanted to keep doing it. We thought this is going well, why stop?'

Of all the bands that You And Me Versus Them played with during those Macclesfield Youth Bands' gigs, their favourite was a Muse tribute act: 'They were called Muesli,' adds Davies, 'which was hilarious. They had a great set-up. The guy playing the piano had a camera hooked up to him. The monitor was on the front of his piano so you could see him playing the keys. It was funny… and what a great name!'

Many years down the line, the band that You And Me Versus Them morphed into – The 1975 – would support the real Muse as their stock began to rise in 2013.

Meanwhile, back at school, being the-kids-in-the-band gave Healy and Co a certain cachet at Wilmslow High, but they themselves were in fact steeped in jealousy over an older band: 'We were *the band* in school, but we wanted to be the band who were in the year above called The Connection Theory – so emo,' Healy later told *Clash* magazine.

With a shared adolescence, the young band essentially grew up together in the same room: a rehearsal room. 'Playing together and growing up together, we've learned each other's strengths and weaknesses,' Adam Hann would later recall in his interview with Tzvi Gluckin. 'Where to rely on each other… and where not to rely on each other!'

'We never really had any careerist ambitions,' Healy later told US radio station FUN 107.1. 'There was such a purity in what we were doing. It was just five people making pop music in a bedroom. When people started to hear it… it's almost like people hearing your diary.'

Few bands that form in school remain intact to reach a level of success. The 1975 are one of the few who've managed it (U2 are another example). Healy has long since held onto the belief that this early bond sets them apart from other bands: 'At that age, you're doing it for immediate reaction, for immediate fun,' he explained to *Coup de Main* magazine. 'You're not doing it because you want to be cool, you're doing it for the same reason you play a video game or play football. Now that idea, that mantra, has never really left us. And that's why we've never really been embraced in the UK by the hipster press. For example, we've been voted as one of the worst bands of the year by the *NME*, and it doesn't really bother us because those kinds of publications and those ideas are based around the frivolous brittle elements that surround music, and not actually about music itself. It's all about what's cool, or what's past, or what's present – whereas that doesn't affect us. We just like making music, and we're lucky that we've been embraced enough to actually just do that.'

As well as pop-punk influences, You And Me Versus Them also sought out the heavier, more challenging sounds of New Yorkers Coheed and Cambria and the intensely musical Dream Theater. Both bands excelled at the kind of super-complex musicality that Healy and Co could only dream of. 'When we were younger… you're making noise for the sake of it,' Daniel would later tell music journalist Nic Harcourt. 'We were a lot heavier. We had original material within a month [of forming]. We were making ambient, progressive rock.'

Their musical interests were diverse, but one common bond was a shared interest in their parents' record collections. Soft-rockers Eagles, the blue-collar rock of Bruce Springsteen, mixed in with the inevitable eighties pop of Eurythmics.

The band would often practise their music in a semi-derelict 'shed' next to Healy's home. That 'shed' became their world – a safe house from the outside world. 'It was the nucleus – it was everything,' Healy would later explain to Radio 1's Huw Stephens. 'It was where we rehearsed, it was where we ate, it was where we slept, it was where we partied. All of the songs were about what happened in that room.'

Owen Davies said, 'It was like a little outhouse, separate to the main building. Matty's mum and dad were great; they gave us free rein. We ended drawing all over it in black biro from head to toe on all the walls and it just became *our* place. So most nights we'd go down there and rehearse, there was no one who didn't want to do it. We all had little jobs on the side and made it work and based everything around the band.'

Guitarist Adam Hann had a job in the nursery department of John Lewis in Cheadle, demonstrating pushchairs and other items. Staff at the store remember Hann talking regularly about his music ambitions and how he hoped to pursue a career outside of nursery products.

'My musical ability wasn't as good as the other guys, definitely' continues Owen. 'The other guys were meticulous, even Adam. I started playing guitar before him but he'd have lessons all the time, every week, and within two years he was blowing people away. Which was remarkable really, I think. When we used to play soundchecks before every gig, you could see how good Adam was, and George on drums. At the time we were sixteen, we were playing gigs with people in their twenties and they were all ridiculously good for their age. In terms of rehearsals though, we were all in the same boat, at least to start with. Pretty much every night after school, we'd go round to Matty's house. We must have annoyed his parents, but we were there all the time.'

In fact, the noise from the 'shed' got so bad that Tim Healy had to have the building sound-proofed. 'All the rehearsals took place at our home, where Matthew spent his formative years,' Denise Welch later told ITV's Lorraine Kelly. 'I was always shouting… "Will you shut up!"'

Welch had enough to deal with at the time – her personal life was generating a great deal of attention in the British tabloid press. She sat the teenage Matthew down and told him that she was about to be splashed across the Sunday newspapers. She'd had an affair with a technician while filming a series in Devon and journalists had got hold of the story.

'I had to face the nightmare of telling my parents and Matthew that I was going to be in the papers,' Welch later wrote in her autobiography, *Pulling Myself Together*. 'Matthew was about fourteen years old at the time, vulnerable and incredibly sensitive, so I found it very hard to tell him. It was easier telling my parents because they already knew about the affair. Matthew was incredibly grown up about it, but he has since said it was a defining moment in his life. It was the moment he realised that his parents weren't gods, but simply two people who had simply fallen in love, got together and had a baby. Tim and I had been through many ups and downs before, but Matthew had not really been aware of any major conflict.'

When the story appeared, the press camped out at the end of Healy's drive, trying to get a photo of his parents as they arrived and left the house. Events like these can't have been easy for the teenager. It's unlikely any of his friends at school – or his newfound band mates – could possibly understand what it was like to be the young Matthew Healy. Perhaps the best form of escape was through music. His school encouraged Matthew's fledgling band, with Wilmslow High's head of music, Gary Morley, cited as being particularly influential in helping them get started.

Healy also gravitated towards a mini sub-culture that had built up around the Urbis centre, close to Victoria train station in Manchester's city centre. The arts and exhibition centre had as much going on outside as it did inside – moshers, goths and skateboarders had all taken up residence on the small grassy area alongside the building. Healy found a 'home' here and would spend hours hanging around outside Urbis. The scene would later disperse somewhat when the arts centre closed down to be replaced by the National Football Museum, but he did once return to the site when he became well-known, to see if anyone remembered him – they did and his presence caused a scene: 'It felt a bit wanky, because I'd done it on purpose,' he confessed to music journalist Laura Barton. 'I undid a button and I think I was probably just being as Matthew Healy as

I could possibly be. It was mental. That's one of the kind of things I do to validate myself.'

After leaving school with two GCSEs, there was work of sorts for Healy – odd jobs in local restaurants – but he seemed to be very much feeling his way in terms of his nascent band, the music he was creating at home in his bedroom and who he was. He would later admit that he only decided he was straight at the age of sixteen: 'I always thought that I love girlie things,' he later told Q magazine. 'I love teen movies, I love the music that is imbued with that. I've always really wanted women around. I've always trusted women. I was always obsessed with my mum's friends. I'm not necessarily a mummy's boy but I've always been comforted by the women in my life.'

He was also happy to take the opportunities to perform that his mum's job gave him. In 2005 he sang at The Lowry theatre in Salford in a show put on by the Wilmslow-based Sargent Academy of Performing Arts, run by Wilmslow High teacher Gill Sargent. Welch acted as compère and both Matthew and his brother, Louis, then just four years old, sang. The older Healy performed 'A Town Called Malice' by The Jam.

As the band reached their mid-to-late teens they would experiment with a number of names – some better than others – that would reflect the sound they were forming. 'To start off, we were called Me And You Versus Them,' says Owen Davies. 'After that it was Forever Drawing Six.' This early incarnation has often, mistakenly, been referred to as 'Forever Enjoying Sex'. 'It definitely wasn't that!' confirms Davies.

'Then obviously we were Drive Like I Do, with the emphasis on the "I" for some reason. Drive Like *I* Do. We played with that name, when I was with them, for a good two years. Once we started recording our own music it was pretty much always under that name.'

I asked Davies what he thought were Drive Like I Do's best songs during this period: '"We Are The Street Fighters", "Shootout At The University Fair",' he states. 'They were Coheed and Cambria, Fall Out Boy kind of songs. They were the bands we looked up to at the time and we did sound very similar to early Fall Out Boy albums. But I thought the songs were good – as I would because I was part of the process! I listen to them once in a blue moon, it's nice. I think at the early stages it was a case of everybody evolving all the time with the sounds. If you were to listen to our early songs – one will be kind of like an early Fall Out Boy song and one will be a heavy Coheed-style song and one will be a proggy song as well. We were always trying different things, sifting through what we did and didn't like.'

Details about these formative years have, until now, tended to be a little sketchy. Fortunately, as well as Owen Davies, we also have eyewitnesses who watched and helped the band in those early years. Manchester-based promoter Ben Hiard came across Matthew Healy and his mates virtually by accident. 'I set up a club night called Pop Bubble Rock, it started in September 2006,' Hiard told me. 'I got into promoting after putting on a gig for my birthday when I was a student. It made me fall in love with promoting. I'd get joy from filling an empty room. I thought it would be fun to mix stuff like Blink-182 with student-friendly pop music. Then I thought, *let's put some live bands on to play before the club night*. This is February 2007. My friends were in a band called The Honeymoon Suite. They had a lot of promise – they were as good as You Me At Six but were two years too early. I put them on the bill but I needed a band to support them. This is back in the days of Myspace – I was trawling through, looking for Manchester bands and I came across this band called Drive Like I Do.'

Hiard liked what he heard and thought the young band would be a good match for The Honeymoon Suite: 'Drive Like I Do had a few rough – *really* rough – home recordings and I just loved it straight away. It was really raw. I loved the singers' voices – it's a lot different to how it is now, very raspy and punky but with pop hooks. That's why I liked it. I think he [Healy] played acoustic guitar and there was a full band behind him. I got in touch via Myspace and invited them to play. It was in Scu Bar, a tiny little basement room off Oxford Road [the main road that cuts through Manchester's student area]. It's a Mormon church now. It was a fiver for the gig and the club night – it wasn't to make money, but because it'd be fun to put on these two bands. There were probably sixty people there – no stage, just the corner of a room. I think they did it for forty quid petrol money.

'And they were great, fantastic – I thought, these guys are brilliant, especially the singer. He was charismatic, he was a proper little emo kid. He had the big hair, the baseball cap – he looked like Ash from Pokémon! He looked like he was going to catch some Pokémon – but everyone looked like that in those days. He looked like we all looked. He didn't look like super-cool world superstars The 1975.'

'At the time, we were super-nerds,' Healy later confirmed in an interview with *SPIN*. 'Loads of bands, when they're seventeen, eighteen, they're like the cool kids and know other bands... We were *not* that.'

'When I first saw them, their talent was undeniable,' Hiard says today. 'There were loads of talented bands out there, but they had something special.'

The Scu Bar gig would be memorable for guitarist Owen Davies for a slightly different reason, though – it marked the beginning of the end for his association with the band. When the gig was arranged, Davies realised that it clashed with the other great love of his life: 'Scu Bar, that was in my latter stages of when I was in the band,' Davies revealed to me. 'I remember that gig in particular. I'm a big fan of Manchester United – the band wasn't my only interest. We were supposed to be playing quite late but I made them change it to earlier because I had a ticket to the United game. I can't image the other guys were too impressed with that at the time. It would have been a 7.45pm kick-off. I made the second half, but looking back, they might not have taken too kindly to it.'

Healy confirms that the feeling was mutual: 'He was trying to leave the band as we were trying to become a four-piece, but weren't letting each other know,' the singer told *Q* magazine in 2016. 'We'd go off and do gigs without him, while he would miss gigs on purpose and then we'd both go, "Oh sorry, damn it!"'

DJ Dan Deighan also saw the band at this very early stage and followed them through their next few incarnations. 'They were a five-piece called Drive Like I Do when I first saw them – it would have been about 2007,' Deighan told me. 'They played at The Phoenix club on Oxford Road. [The Phoenix was knocked down in summer 2016.] It was in the upstairs bar. It was a pop-punk night but they also played cheesy pop – people don't go there to act cool. It's OK if a punk band sounds a bit poppy – and that's exactly what Drive Like I Do were. They were like a punk band – they had some really heavy songs with a pop element. I think they were influenced by American pop-punk bands like Green Day, Blink-182. You could see their influences, it shone through.'

Drive Like I Do clearly took a shine to The Phoenix and played there several times: 'We put them on again at The Phoenix,' recalled Ben Hiard to me. 'That would have been later in 2007. A few more people seemed to know about them – again they were fantastic. We did a beach-party theme with different stuff on different floors. Drive Like I Do literally played on the pub floor. Sonic Boom Six played, Failsafe from Lancashire played, Drive Like I Do played. They did it for a crate of cider. It was one of my fondest memories of them.'

For former guitarist Davies one of the highlights of his time with the band was playing an unsigned bands' night at the Academy 3 venue in Manchester. 'I've still got the show times poster here on my wall,' he says. 'A fair few people were there to see us. I'll always remember that as being something special because it was a pretty big crowd, all listening to our music – it was a nice experience.'

Dan Deighan told me: 'I saw them again downstairs at The Scream bar [downstairs at The Phoenix] – it was a Pop Bubble Rock's birthday party. There were only about twenty people watching. There was no stage, they were on the floor of the bar. There was one lad who was steaming drunk; he was heckling them. Matthew handled it really well. He already had the stage presence to deal with it.'

His interest piqued by what he'd seen, Deighan tried to find out more about Drive Like I Do, but following the group would sometimes prove difficult in those early years – they would post songs and videos online then remove them swiftly. They seemed shadowy, mysterious. These early attempts at creating a buzz would resurface later in their career. 'They were always very mystical on Myspace, even back then,' Deighan says. 'You wouldn't get much from them, all very short and sweet. Everyone was trying to find out what was going on with them. They'd put a song online then delete it. It was all very cryptic from day one – but so well thought out. Extremely clever.'

Maybe it *was* cryptic. Deleting things from the Internet was a trick they'd use to great effect in the future. But maybe there was another explanation for the band's mysterious low-key online presence: 'We were lazy,' Healy said in an interview with *Guitar Sessions*. 'We were stoners in a band, we didn't release things on the Internet, we didn't have a history. There was no awareness.'

The sense of anonymity was eased when the band managed to get themselves invited on to Annie Mac's night-time show on Radio 1. Drive Like I Do was invited on as part of an unsigned bands' slot. It was one of several tantalising tastes of what things could be like – as with many other events that seemed like breakthroughs at the time, nothing in particular came of it. Owen Davies: 'We had a few of these dangling carrots – something like that would come along and then we'd have the kind of excitement, then a few months would go by, then nothing. It was just so hard trying to get somewhere. It's not why I left, but I think it contributed. We had a message off McFly on Myspace as well, saying they were possibly interested in us doing some shows with them – nothing came of it. Obviously all these little things add up.'

In the end, they added up to Owen Davies and the band deciding to go their separate ways. 'The funny thing is, we never really spoke of it,' he told me, when I tracked him down in 2016. 'It was a mutual thing, definitely. I wasn't 100 per cent committed to it after a few years – they were committed, obviously. Nothing was said, there was literally no conversation. I think I made it clear to the guys that I wanted to go back to uni and they just kept going without me, basically. But there was never a sit-down conversation with anyone storming out of rooms or anything. Music was always kind of a hobby for me and they were wanting to stick at it and go full whack with it.

'I'd tried it [university], I'd gone to Salford University for a year, left after one year to focus on the band – I did audio and video technology, but there were as many days I just stayed at home and spent more time with the band. Sometimes I'd only go twice, three times a week. I thought, after a few years with the band, it's not really what I want to do all the time. I wanted to tick off the proverbial bucket list.'

It's tempting to caricature Davies as a Pete Best figure – Best being the drummer who parted company with The Beatles just before they became successful. But try as I might to ask him in different ways whether he made the right decision or not, Davies is adamant he has no regrets: 'No, not at all, never crosses my mind. The only thing I say is I'm personally so happy for the guys, 'cos I know how much effort they put into it from day one. The blood, sweat and tears they spilt to get where they are. I still went to their gigs after I left – I remember going in 2008 to Leeds to see them – there's never been any bad blood or animosity or anything like that. I don't class myself as being in The 1975 because I wasn't, as they never had that name and they never had that music when I was there. I was very much Drive Like I Do, which is almost a different band – though obviously with the same members. But if you listen to one song and a 1975 song, you wouldn't think it was the same band, would you?'

Meanwhile, the band tightened their sound to accommodate their new four-piece status. Then, out of the blue, they got an email from someone who had seen their Myspace page and wanted to meet them. Matthew Healy later said: 'Jamie [Oborne] turned up in his BMW and his Barbour jacket and said, "I want to manage you. I think you guys could be one of the biggest bands in the world".'

THREE

THE BIG
SLOWDOWN
LIKE I DO

As well as their rehearsal shed next to Healy's house, Drive Like I Do had another spot they used as a meeting place and hang-out. This being Cheshire, the place they chose was a French café in Wilmslow town centre, Petit Delice at the Grove Arcade. Healy liked it so much he would later name it as one of his top-five favourite restaurants in the world – and by that time he'd seen a fair bit of the world: 'From the ages of seventeen to twenty-three, when we were trying to get signed, we'd eat at this place every day. Retrospectively, we're a bit annoyed they never gave us anything free, because I'm not exaggerating how much we ate there.'

It's easy to imagine them sitting in Petit Delice discussing the email they'd received from ex-musician Jamie Oborne showing interest in the band. It sounded too good to be true

– Healy was initially cautious. He wanted to know how much Oborne was planning to charge them for being their manager. 'This was a grown-up,' Healy explained later to Radio 1. 'We'd been through no processes of qualification. We'd been validated by no one apart from my dad. So to have somebody who clearly had more than thirty quid telling us that we were gonna be a massive band… we believed him.'

After his own musical ambitions went awry, Jamie Oborne had gone to university, where in the early noughties he'd started a music management company with a friend. When the partnership ended he decided to go it alone and formed his own company. Perhaps he found a kinship with the lottery scratchcard-loving lads of The 1975 through a shared interest in taking a chance: he called the company All On Red.

Oborne racked up an early success with Yorkshire band One Night Only, best known for their 2007 hit, 'Just For Tonight'. Lead singer George Craig briefly became a tabloid target after he was linked with actress Emma Watson. A fan of the band contacted Oborne via Myspace to tell him that he might like Drive Like I Do. And Oborne did. 'We were amazed that he found us,' Healy later told US-based radio and TV presenter Nic Harcourt. 'There were no pictures of us online, we were very ambiguous – very happy playing shows to nobody in Manchester and being a kind of hipster band. He turned up and said he wanted to manage us – and he stuck with us for seven years while we did nothing. And he looked after us.'

It would be the start of a long and sometimes frustrating

relationship between the band and their manager. 'It got to the point where the band were sick of listening to promises that never came off,' Oborne later admitted in an interview during Belfast Music Week. '[When the band started to get attention] people on Twitter were saying how they had blown up out of nowhere – but it's like, fuck, if only you knew the amount of manpower and money that went into that artist [beforehand] you wouldn't be saying that.'

'He's really nurtured us as a band since we met,' Healy told *musicOMH* video channel. 'We've always believed we had the potential to do big things with this band, it was just important for us to do it our own way and not to rush anything.'

No one could be accused of rushing things. Oborne began the long and ultimately fruitless task of trying to get the band signed – and of looking after their interests, particularly that of their lead singer: 'Matthew Healy is not going to get another job,' Oborne admitted in an interview with *Music Business Worldwide* nearly ten years after he first met the frontman. 'He's not built for that life, so I have to make sure that he gets what he needs. I know it sounds like a joke but it's not, it's really serious. I didn't want to be just another manager. I wanted to focus on development and build a business that had assets, like a record company – with the artists sharing in the creation of that asset wealth.'

Meanwhile, as his band became more fully formed, so too did Healy's interest in the rock 'n' roll lifestyle. There was little Matthew could do by way of teenage rebellion when it came to wild living – mum Denise has been open about her use of cocaine to counteract the effects of her depression, even snorting the drug in her dressing room at Granada TV – but he had a go nonetheless. He would later describe himself as a 'junkie' when asked about drugs by the *Guardian*: 'I wasn't a heroin addict – I never lost it to heroin – but I was a coke addict big-time. I was eighteen, I dabbled in everything. I wanted to be Jack Kerouac. I thought I was as decadent as all of that. I thought: the world will catch up.'

Healy's dabbling in drugs would seem quite tame when mum Denise published her autobiography around the same time. In *Pulling Myself Together*, the actress – now even more famous, thanks to her appearances on ITV's *Loose Women* – talked about her private life with toe-curling honesty. As well as her post-natal depression after giving birth to Matthew, she outlined her drinking, affairs and drug taking. The book featured photos of Healy as a baby and as a young teenager. It can't have been easy for him, as he approached his twenty-first birthday, to have so much of his parents' lives exposed to public scrutiny. But according to Welch, her son has taken it in his stride: 'Once I asked him about my drinking,' she wrote. '"Obviously all kids hate their parents getting pissed because it's so boring," he said. "But I wouldn't change you for the world. I like the fact that my life has been a bit rock 'n' roll, because it's made me who I am."'

Meanwhile, drummer George Daniel had enrolled on a music production course and immersed himself in ambient music, electronic and drum loops. The techniques he learned in college began to seep into the band's music. 'We've never been a guitar-driven, jam-an-idea-in-a-room kind of band,' he later explained in an interview with *Guitar Sessions*. 'We've always worked in a more programmed way, starting on a laptop. One microphone, Logic [Pro] and a shit load of samples.'

Slowly, the band began to appear on the radars of more promoters. Manchester events manager Ben Taylor was one of them: 'They were called Drive Like I Do when I first met them. Probably 2010, maybe even earlier. I played a show with them with one of my bands at the Academy 3 – a Manchester unsigned night. You see a band sometimes and you think, *They've got something*. They had songs that I remembered after I'd left the venue – and for an unsigned band, you don't get that very often. It made me want to work with them again and again. There was something about them. They looked good. They were cocky but in a good way. They had songs like "Chocolate". There were songs that have travelled with them, and "Chocolate" was definitely one of them.'

'"Robbers", "Chocolate" and "Sex" – we spent a long time playing them, trying to get them right,' Healy would later tell *Atwood* magazine. 'They were shit for a while, but they're good now. We came up with the title for the song "Sex" first. I was like, "We're going to have a song called 'Sex'," and then we wrote it from there. What was on my mind? Trying to get off with a girl, I imagine. Trying to persuade a girl to go for me instead of him. The simple, classic tale of being seventeen.'

The people who spoke to me about this stage in the band's development all told me that one of the things that stuck out about the band was how pleasant they were to deal with. They played well, then hung around, watched the other bands, had a drink and had a laugh. Events manager Ben Taylor: 'There's not many bands from back then I can even remember, but they were always up for a chat. Bands like that stick in your head. Back then everyone wanted to be Oasis, with the swagger. To have a band that were actually nice – you could count them on one hand. So I built up a bit of a relationship with them… through all their name changes!'

Meanwhile, Drive Like I Do were by now securing bottom-of-the-bill slots at larger venues in Manchester, with bigger acts like 100 Reasons. The show was promoted by Ben Hiard, who was still keeping tabs on Drive Like I Do. 'It was a comeback tour for 100 Reasons. I'd always liked them and this was going to be a big gig.'

Healy would later cite 100 Reasons' 2002 album *Ideas Above Our Station* as one of his Top 10 releases: '[It] came out at a time when a lot of UK rock bands were copying the American popcorn sounds,' he would later explain to *Louder Than War*. '*Ideas Above Our Station* came out and it had all those major chord progressions and had a really life-affirming sound, and it felt like it was coming from a really British perspective and I really related to that.'

It must have seemed like a massive leap forward for the band to appear on the same bill as 100 Reasons – promoter Ben

Hiard remembers the gig well: 'Johnny Foreigner supported. It was seven pounds. Ridiculous. It was a 700-capacity venue, we probably had 800 there. People would have thrown money at me to play on that bill. I rang up Matthew and said, "This gig is happening. I really want you guys to play." It blew his mind! He said, "I love 100 Reasons, they're one of my favourite bands... Are you sure?" He was really excited. At that point they may have had a booking agent but it was all very informal, direct contact.'

The band were now posting videos online as Drive Like I Do but still weren't recognisable as the group that would become The 1975. The pop-punk influence was definitely waning: 'I think that we made a conscious decision to become more pop, which in turn is less pop,' Healy would later try to explain to *Spook* magazine, 'because pop-punk, by the end, was *so* poppy, culturally and musically. But, yeah, we got rid of the punk ethos. We just grew up, man. You don't still listen to [US emo punk band] Taking Back Sunday every day, do you? I think what really happened is that, as the primary songwriter at the time... How do I explain it? I grew up on black music, soul music, Otis Redding, Michael Jackson. When I was, like, sixteen/seventeen we realised we didn't have to be alternative, we don't need to *only* embrace rock bands. Why don't we play funk music, or soul music, and see what happens when we try and do that?'

As the music began to change, a greater interest in the visual aspect of their performance was also starting to creep in. 'A week before the 100 Reasons gig Matthew messaged me and said, "Can I bring a bit of lightning with me?"' recalled Ben Hiard. 'He wanted to bring a strobe light. He said, "We're trying something new, it's just for one of the songs." They played a very atmospheric song and during the song this strobe light started pulsing behind the drummer – that's the closest link I can find between them then, and now. The idea of an aesthetic. His mum and dad were at the gig – loads of his family too. To me, it was a turning point. But immediately after that gig Drive Like I Do seemed to fizzle out – they supported a few bands but then they seemed to go quiet. The next thing I knew they came back with the new name.'

Soon after, they played the city's Ruby Lounge venue as Drive Like I Do, then changed their name to Big Sleep, believing they'd outgrown their old moniker. The number of names the band have gone under are many and various – Healy claims they played one run of shows and changed their name every night, at one stage introducing themselves as The David Henderson Experience, named after an exceptionally quiet pupil in his class. 'People talk about the name changes a lot, because people are interested in our band now,' Healy told *FaceCulture*. 'People weren't interested in our band when we were changing names. Our first name was with us from about sixteen, so when you get to nineteen you think that's not really us. So we changed to Big Sleep.'

Again, we're grateful to Dan Deighan for being on the spot when the name changes happened, looking out for any major differences: 'They played as Big Sleep in January 2010 at Sound Control – there weren't many people there for that one. It was almost as if they didn't want their name to get out there too much – like they were still trying to find their way a bit. They had family and friends there – and people who knew about them – maybe thirty or forty people.'

Ben Taylor told me, 'By early 2010 you could tell they were taking it a bit more seriously. You thought, something might be happening here. They always had a good local fan base. They always brought loads of people to the shows, so promoters wanted them on the bill.'

Ben Hiard: 'The first time I saw them as Big Sleep they'd released a video on YouTube called *Ghosts* in conjunction with a music magazine. [The video had been shot in the Healys' shed.] That's when I thought, hang on a minute, there's money and management behind this. Someone who knows what they're doing.'

The marimba-led bounce of 'Ghosts' would be the song that sticks in people's minds from this period. Many couldn't understand why the ultra-catchy, Paul Simonesque tune didn't transfer over when they became The 1975. 'They put up a track called "Ghosts" when they were called Big Sleep,' Ben Taylor told me. 'It was hard to find stuff online – the Drive Like I Do stuff had gone. I tried to play someone the track… and that had gone too! Then I was told, nah, they're called The Slowdown now.'

George Daniel would later describe this period as, 'the dark phase of the band; the only time we questioned the future of what we were doing.' He told the BBC, 'It's a period when we were being quite attention seeking. We were pursuing a record deal and we wrote a song ["Ghosts"] with the purpose of getting those kind of people's attention... whether or not it was true to ourselves. At the time we were really enjoying it, but we grew out of it really quickly.'

It would seem suicidal for any band to keep changing their name so often – either they had something to hide or they couldn't make up their minds who they were. 'By all rights they shouldn't have made it,' states Hiard. 'They kept changing their name! It seemed disorganised. And to do it three or four times... Maybe it was genius marketing!'

Ben Taylor again: 'Within twelve months they moved between those three names. I thought, is this going to be an ongoing thing, are they going to keep changing their name? I thought Big Sleep was a great name. Slowdown had kind of been done a million times in Manchester. The Slowdown did an afternoon show for us as at the Academy 3 as part of Pop Bubble Rock with a band called The Maple State. You could tell something was going on. There were more people involved. They were dressing more like a gang. It looked a bit more... official. More real.'

The Maple State would have a surprising influence on Healy as a frontman – he was watching closely what other bands were doing and adding them to his wish list of how he wanted to come across as a performer: 'I used to love this little band called The Maple State,' Healy told journalist Michael Hann. 'I remember seeing them at the Academy 3 in Manchester. There couldn't have been more than ten people there, but in my head there were about 35,000. The guitarist did a move where he turned round and pointed at me – it meant so much to me that I'm still talking about it! When you become part of the show, when the lead singer or the guitarist invites you in, you never forget it.'

His stagecraft may have been improving, but Healy still had issues with his band's name – issues that were about to come to a head. 'We thought, *This is quite a cool name*,' Healy said about their choice of Big Sleep. 'Then we signed a small record deal in America [with Vagrant] and they said, "You know there's an American band called The Big Sleep?" No one really knew who we were – *we* didn't really know who we were – so we didn't really care. Let's change the name again, this'll be fun! So then we were The Slowdown.'

'None of them were genuine,' recalls George Daniel. 'Even Big Sleep – it's a great name, it's got a good feel, but it's a bit dark. Same with The Slowdown – none of them had a genuine reason. All band names become detached then they become the band's name.'

Again, promoter Ben Hiard managed to work out that this 'new' band were in fact Matthew Healy and friends and put them on with London band Tellison – though they clearly didn't make that much of an impression on the headliners; they're listed on the Tellison website as being called The

Slowdive. 'I put them on as The Slowdown – a Sunday-night gig with a London indie punk band called Tellison. I arranged it really quickly and got them on because I'd heard Matthew and the others were playing music again. There were four bands on the bill – The Cape Race and Ghosts Saddles were the others – and they were the second band on. They weren't major billing. They turned up and they had more of an eighties poppy sound than before – but still raw. I remember Matthew wasn't wearing band T-shirts with floppy hair any more. He had an open shirt on; his style had definitely changed. They turned up looking hungover as hell – but as soon as they started playing, they were tight. I'd never seen a band like them. They were the perfect mix of raw… and knowing what the fuck they were doing. They were slick but it seemed really pure. Six pounds to get in. How times have changed. That was the last time I put them on. After that… astronomical.'

The Slowdown didn't seem to be gaining much traction as a name – not least within the band themselves: 'We waited a few months and then we thought, *We don't really like that name*,' says Healy. 'People were like, you can't keep changing the name of the band all the time! We were like, why? Only a few people know who we are.'

Other names like Talkhouse barely got further than the ideas board – though it would be used as a name for Matthew and George's more leftfield ideas. Healy's mum Denise suggested they call themselves No Added Sugar. That didn't get far either.

Meanwhile the search for a 'genuine' name continued until

Matthew Healy went on a break to Mallorca: 'I met an artist on holiday,' he told *Some Kind of Awesome*. 'It sounds a bit more bohemian, idealistic than maybe it was but I met him and ended up leaving with a book that must have been treated almost like a diary by a previous owner, so when I read it there was all these mad scribblings and notes, and the person had dated it "the 1st of June The 1975". Then when it came to naming the band it just seemed like quite an appropriate title, you know.'

The artist in question was Nottinghamshire-born painter David Templeton, who's known for his collages and pictures of Elvis Presley. Healy had the book in his possession for eighteen months before he'd actually read it. What struck him most was the curious placing of 'The' in front of the year. 'At the time I just thought that the word "The" preceding a date was a strong use of language,' he later explained to the *Guardian*. 'I never thought it would be something that would later come to be so important. When it came to naming the band, it was perfect.'

Healy took the name back to the band – originally saying he planned to use it for a slightly vague electronic side-project he was planning. The first thing they noticed was that it took a lot longer to say it than it did to recognise it. George Daniel: 'I always said initially that I thought it looked amazing written down, but that it might have been too long – it's seven syllables.'

As well as having a surplus of syllables, The-Nine-Teen-Se-Ven-Tee-Five also broke some other cardinal rules of rock band names. Very few acts at that time were called 'The' and with a management and a publishing deal now in place, this wasn't seen to be the time to start experimenting with daft names. But Healy was adamant – and went about sealing the deal in a characteristically flamboyant fashion. 'The publishers said absolutely no way are you calling the band The 1975,' he later told *FaceCulture*. 'It's too long and there's never been a big band that's just been numbers. So we looked at each other and went… *that's the name*. So I went out and got it tattooed on my arm that same day and I sent them a photo of it. As soon as they said, "there's never been a big band, that's just numbers", we thought that's it, The 1975 is our name. It's not because other names didn't come around. That's the definitive name.'

FOUR

FACEDOWN SEX

The start of 2012 – the year that his band would truly start to break through – would be an extremely trying time for Matthew Healy. It's amazing he managed to get so much done and focus on the band at all. 'My band took off, my family fell apart,' is how he himself would succinctly put it.

In the first week of January his mum Denise had entered the *Big Brother* house to take part in the notorious reality show that had transferred from its traditional home on Channel 4 to Channel 5 the year before. Her reasons for doing the show were brutally simple – a massive tax bill meant the family might have to sell their home in Alderley Edge. For Matthew, still living at home at the time, this was serious stuff – if nothing else it would spell the end of the shed and its cocoon-like importance for the band. Welch's way to avoid having to sell up was to take up the offer from the *Big Brother* producers to join the likes of MC Romeo from So Solid Crew, *X Factor* hopeful Frankie Cocozza and actor Michael Madsen in the televised house. Healy was dead against the idea from the start and was especially upset to watch his mum's run-ins with other housemates, especially Madsen.

Not only did Welch not take her son's advice, she won the show that year. She later claimed that Matthew didn't want to be in the audience when she left the *Big Brother* house as winner, because he didn't want to be associated with being the son of a *Big Brother* winner, especially as he was, according to her, on the verge of signing a record deal. In fact, it wasn't until she came out of the house that she discovered how much the experience had upset him: 'It was only then that I fully realised what absolute hell Matthew had been through while I was in the house,' she later wrote in her autobiography. 'It was far worse than I had anticipated and he was traumatised by my experience. He'd been on the phone to the *Big Brother* producers every day and had spoken daily to my manager. Twice he'd said that he wanted to pull me out of the house but they had cajoled him and persuaded him against it. He really struggled for me in there. It was so hard for him.'

To make matters worse, also immediately after she left the *Big Brother* house – Welch was now one of the most famous women in Britain – a story appeared in a Sunday tabloid that she'd been having an 'affair' with a PR manager fifteen years her junior called Lincoln Townley. Just before taking part in

Big Brother, Healy's parents had in fact agreed to separate, but were waiting for the right moment to tell Matthew and his brother. Now he'd found out via the press.

Welch then went on *Loose Women* on 6 February to confirm the split live on air. Despite so much of his family's life being played out in public, Healy would later put a positive spin on things: 'It's kinda good – no good marriage ever ended in divorce,' he later reasoned to the *Guardian*. 'If two people had a really good thing going on and they had to get divorced, that would be really sad. But that's never happened once. That's fine. That was a long time coming. Last year [2012] I went on tour and they sold the house. I went home for two days to move out of my house. So I left and I've not really been home since. But I've fucking embraced it, man. Because you take the good with the bad. I don't have a home, but I have a thousand people come and see me, whatever city I'm in. If you can't feel at home there, where can you feel at home?'

In May, Healy's grandmother Annie died. She'd had multiple battles with cancer over the years and she passed away on Denise Welch's birthday, surrounded by her family. 'She was the bravest woman I have ever known; Debbie [Welch's sister], Dad and all of her grandchildren will miss her more than anything, but we are happy knowing she is free from pain,' Denise wrote on her Twitter page. 'She was the best mum and Nanna in the world and will always be in our hearts. May 22nd will forever be a day to celebrate my birthday and the life of this remarkable mum and Nanna.'

Healy, who already had a reasonable collection of tattoos, including one in tribute to his favourite book, *Queer* by William Burroughs, decided that this was the time to get another one. 'My Nanna hated all my tattoos,' Healy later told the Shazam radio show. 'She made me promise that I'd never get a tattoo of her when she died. Then about sixteen hours after she died, I got a tattoo of her on my chest.'

With all this going on – a huge amount for any young person to deal with – perhaps hard work was the ideal distraction. It may have even contributed to the huge steps the band made throughout the year; that, plus a sense of bloody-minded independence: 'We never wanted to be a big band,' Healy claimed in an interview with *Spotlight Report*. 'Then loads of labels started getting interested – and we thought, maybe we *could* be a big band. Then those labels turned us down and told us we weren't right. So then we thought, let's do it ourselves. So we put out the first record and did it ourselves and that's proven to be the best way of doing it.'

A pattern had developed in the band's relations with the record-company establishment – representatives would meet the band, wine and dine them, tell them they had something that was marketable... then, just as it came to signing, the labels would change their minds, saying it wasn't *quite* right... Thanks, but no thanks.

'When we were Big Sleep, we put out a video, our first song called "Ghosts" and we got a lot of attention, like a lot of industry attention,' Healy would later explain to journalists when the band visited Manila in 2014. 'And then they came to our house to meet us, and they heard half of what is now the album. Now that album is quite strange. And I think when you work for a record label and you've heard one song, and then you go meet a band and every other song sounds totally different, you're all scared. They didn't like the idea. And we were saying, "Well, no, that's the way that our generation consumes music. It's good to have a band that creates music like that." They weren't happy with that idea, so we didn't get signed. And then, we just did it ourselves. And we kind of made a plan, a plan that is still working.'

After being turned down by every record company in the country – none of whom could see the potential in songs written by the band that would later become hits – the band's manager, Jamie Oborne, decided to set up his own record label, Dirty Hit, to release their material. The 1975 remain a Dirty Hit act to this day – they really are an 'indie' band in the truest sense of the word. Being on an independent would give them an astonishing degree of creative freedom in a record company landscape filled with bands trying desperately to appeal to a mass market, whatever compromises that entails. The decision to put out their own material essentially secured the short-term future of the band – their parents were fast running out of patience with what probably seemed like a pipe dream of being in a successful band: 'We were *just* running out of time with our parents,' George Daniel later told radio presenter Nic Harcourt. 'It went from, *What's happening with the band?* to, *What are you going to do when it doesn't happen?* It was literally in the nick of time.'

By the time they officially became The 1975 in January 2012, they already had an album's worth of songs. But instead of releasing that, they decided to save it, opting instead to release a series of EPs to generate interest in the band. Oborne also signed York singer-songwriter Benjamin Francis Leftwich, who would chart with his first album, *Last Smoke Before The Snowstorm*, in 2011. Leftwich would, like The 1975, also release a set of EPs prior to his debut album. The trailblazer for the EPs-first technique, though, was Ed Sheeran, who'd put out a set of five EPs before releasing his debut album in 2011. It had worked out pretty well for Sheeran so why not for Healy, Daniel, Hann and MacDonald?

'What we wanted to do,' guitarist Hann later explained to *The Rave* video channel, 'was give people a wealth of material so they could understand what the band was all about, before we came along with a full-length album. The EPs were an entry point.'

'People have made the understandable assumption that our material has worked chronologically,' Healy would later explain to *Music OMH* about the decision to hold back on some of their material. 'For example, we wrote [EPs] *Facedown*, then *Sex*, then *Music For Cars*, etc. That's not actually how it happened. We wrote our album first. When we came to releasing music, we wanted to provide people with a real wealth of material that depicted exactly what we were about. So people could get to know us like you get to know a person, learning more and more over time.'

While preparing to release the first of the EPs, the band were booked to play a gig that would prove to be a pivotal event in their story. In the early summer of 2012, Ben Taylor was events manager at Sound Control in Manchester. Taylor had been aware of The 1975 – in their various incarnations – for nearly three years. There was a sense that interest in Matthew Healy's 'new' band was growing and he wanted them to play at the venue's new room. 'In July 2012, I approached their agent about The 1975 doing a show,' Taylor told me. 'We wanted to do it in our 150-capacity room. It was to be part of a tour – only a small run of shows.'

Taylor noticed straight away that the band and their approach had become a little slicker than when he'd dealt with them previously. Though everyone had liked Healy and his mates, they were sometimes a little ramshackle. Now, things had changed: they had a unified look, a collective attitude, an aesthetic. 'They gave me "assets" [a digital package of photos and graphics]. Big Sleep and Slowdown didn't get as far as that. They never had this before. Drive Like I Do maybe had a font that they used, The Slowdown didn't.'

The black-and-white look of the 'assets' sent to Taylor reflected the band's newly sharpened sense of how they should come across. 'Well, we are big fans of fashion and film – I think most people are, aren't they?' Healy explained to journalist Darragh Faughey a few months after the first EP's release. 'But we wanted to reflect our love for those things through what we were doing. We haven't actively searched for a visual identity really. We just know what's right for us, what looks good, and agree upon it. The black and white was really a mood thing. Our music is laden with classic pop sensibilities and major melodies – we try and make our sound quite life-affirming and grand, I suppose. So it's nice to counteract that with an aesthetic that is more melancholic, perhaps – also more removed from reality.'

Used to seeing Healy and friends play to a few dozen people, Taylor also noticed that this time around, things were a little different on the sales front: 'It sold like that,' he recalls, clicking his fingers. 'I think they'd been played on the radio. Huw Stephens had played them on Radio 1. The bill was The 1975, a local band called The Last Party and Catfish and the Bottlemen. They [the Bottlemen] opened up. No fee, they were just happy to play!'

Huw Stephens had played what the band thought was one of their strongest tracks – called 'The City' – as part of a late-night feature about British record label Dirty Hit. The 1975 were introduced as something the label had 'coming up later in the year'. Manager Oborne was interviewed by Stephens, describing them as 'Talking Heads meets M83'. 'They're from Manchester,' Oborne told the Radio 1 presenter, when asked about the band's background.

'We were all sort of sat round the radio to listen to it,' Hann recalled. 'It was [from] 11.30 to midnight… it was late. We sat round together to listen to him play the song and it was a weird feeling. We'd heard the song before but it was like you wanted to make sure it sounded alright on the radio.'

After releasing 'Sex' as a teaser track – accompanied by no information as to who was behind the track – the band went overground with the first of a series of EPs to set out their stall. 'The EPs all have a lead track,' Healy would explain to *musicOMH*. 'On *Facedown* it's "The City" and on *Sex* it's "Sex", obviously, and "Chocolate" is the lead track on *Music For Cars*. It's interesting because we've taken tracks off our album to use as lead tracks on our EPs – as opposed to taking lead tracks off our EPs to use as singles on the album. Each EP has been written around a part of the album – taking an important moment in the story and extending and embellishing it.'

Hann would later explain to the BBC about the background to the first EP: 'We already had the song "The City", which had been knocking around for a while. We all went down to London and took some loose ideas we had knocking around for the other tracks into a studio. It was like a room attached to a church – it had kind of a weird vibe and it was very dark. We wanted to establish a dark aesthetic for the band. The songs on that EP are far less mainstream than the songs on the album.'

The first of the EPs – *Facedown* – was released in the first week of August. 'Facedown', the title track, is a tinkling, dreamy vocoder-thon – it's so processed, layered and dense, it's hard to tell what's going on. Knowing what we know now, it's still very clearly The 1975, and the track wouldn't feel out of place on the band's second album. It's a palate cleanser, a warm-up, designed to get you ready for the *boom boom pow* of 'The City'. A heavy, gated drum loop and a grinding synth bassline herald the lead track of the EP and a chance to hear Healy's voice properly. It's a slight shock for the first-time listener – he may have lived in Cheshire most of his life (via the northeast) but his voice is pure Thames Estuary, a strange yelping mix of Robert Smith of The Cure, Blur's Damon Albarn at his most Mockney, and Peter Gabriel. At times he even sounds like arch cockney Gary Holton, the late lead singer of Heavy Metal Kids, who, as an actor, worked alongside Healy's dad Tim in *Auf Wiedersehen, Pet*.

Healy's voice is backed by a soundscape of repetitive riffs, bleeps and loops that seem culled from a lost Talk Talk album from the eighties. It's a terrific way for the band to outline their intentions after so many years of frustration and name changes – this is a war, not a fight, so if you're not on board please leave the battlefield now. More synths pile in, then a sparse three-note riff from Hann tops it off. It's huge yet simple, and sounded like nothing else of its time. Having said that, to some ears it sounded a lot like Scritti Politti, Tears For Fears and any number of 1980s acts who were big on hair, drums and ideas thirty years earlier, but not a lot like a bunch of young lads from Cheshire in 2012.

Next track 'Antichrist' sounds like a different band again, with – initially, at least – a different singer. The drums are still set to bombast and MacDonald's bass is a subsonic growl. The track has a whiff of Peter Gabriel's late seventies and early eighties run of self-titled albums about it, before it decides to come on a bit U2 at the climax. 'I think it's a great song,' Hann would later reflect. 'But I think that it's something we would never write again – it's just a bit weird.'

Final track 'Woman' is another tone piece – no real rhythm, just sounds – as Healy's voice floats over to the sparest of backing. Just when you think drummer Daniel is about to flex his muscles and go *boom dada boom* again, it's gone. Taking the EP as a whole, it's a baffling yet beguiling mix – without lead track 'The City' it is almost completely and wilfully uncommercial and self-serving, and would probably have left the band doomed to hover around the muso backwaters of late-night niche radio for as long as they chose to.

Reviewers – the few that did review it – were largely impressed, if a little perplexed. Acts from Bloc Party to Foals, via Jeff Buckley, were cited by music journalists trying to get a handle on what they were hearing. 'Someone still makes music like this?' wondered *Pitchfork*, a quote from a largely positive review that would make its way into the critic-baiting video for 'The Sound' a few years down the line. 'It's a muddle, but a promising one… They've been playing together for a decade… It makes sense that they're musically together, but still grasping for their sense of self – all the attendant trappings of being The 1975 are still yet to be sorted out… they'll continue to be a band worth checking for if they decide not to fool themselves.'

'The singer's voice is a little bit whiney,' said music website

Sputnik. 'While the basic songwriting is solid, it's the flourishes and instrumental beauty that lift the band up from just another indie band to one worth watching, and if they deviate from that they could find themselves limited. Still, *Facedown* is a generally gorgeous EP that will appeal to anyone who enjoys ambient pop music.'

But music site *1883* – perhaps bonded with a shared love of year-based names – was definitely on board: 'Soft romance and delicate lyrics are woven deep within the fabric of sound that The 1975 have crafted, making them one of the most emotive new bands around. A slight swagger, floppy haircuts and a common twang in their vocals, The 1975 has all the makings of a promising young band. Oozing confidence and a musical grasp that's matured further than their age range, the band's command is that of a much more experienced group. A small snippet of the band's ability, *Facedown* hints at anthemic choruses and whimpering ballads to come from the four-piece.'

The band's first EP was released at a time when the Manchester music scene was in a state of flux. Such was the reputation of the city's musical heritage that it was now attracting huge numbers of visitors and students keen to tap into the legacy that bands like The Smiths, New Order and Oasis had created. Greater Manchester has the largest student population of any city in Europe and many students were signing up to the area's universities so that they could join bands and get involved in the local gig circuit that The

1975 were already a part of. Manchester was awash with bands who weren't really from Manchester at all. The biggest new 'Manchester' band to have broken through at the time were probably Everything Everything. They'd formed at Salford University but were actually from Northumberland, Kent and Guernsey. Only The Courteeners from Middleton could claim to have been a 'proper' Manchester band who had come through in recent years, but they were an act that were seen as bigger in their home city than elsewhere.

But at the same time as people were being drawn to the city for its musical history, a slight resentment was felt by others about the expectation that being a 'Manchester band' could place on a group of musicians. Some bands – The 1975 included – didn't want to be put against the 'heritage' groups of yesteryear, they wanted to be judged on their own merits.

The city's music scene was a crowded place, with bands elbowing each other to get noticed. In 2012, when *Facedown* was released, what was the nature of the Manchester scene and who were the bands The 1975 were up against?

'Around about that time there were lots of things around Manchester that were grabbing my attention,' music journalist and producer Emily Brinnand told me – she would write one of the first major pieces about The 1975. 'There was a band called Embers who were really great and everyone was raving about them. So they were certainly on my radar. You had bands like Delphic. MONEY as well. PINS – they seemed to be gathering at similar times. Egyptian Hip Hop as well. And as we know, all these people know each other. And they all came from outside of Manchester in the suburbs… Marple, Wilmslow, Bramhall. MONEY had met at uni in Manchester. It was really interesting that all these bands were having a bit of attention, a bit of heat around them all at the same time and that they were coming from the suburbs into the city. So they were the focus around 2012 for me.'

Meanwhile, work was well underway for the band's debut album. Belfast-born Mike Crossey was brought in to produce – he'd carved out a reputation for working well with hungry young acts champing at the bit to put out their first material, having worked with Arctic Monkeys and Jake Bugg. Crossey initially worked on two tracks for the band's second EP – 'Sex' and 'You' – before getting stuck into the album proper. 'Mike was the first producer we met that had ever really wanted to embrace the production we had done previously, and at this stage I had never had that sort of validation as a producer,' George Daniel later explained to music website *iZotope*. '[Previously] I'd done most of the material myself, but they always just felt like we were putting out demos. Mike's input would always be far more scientific than ours. He'd easily spot the frequencies that were contributing too much or too little to an arrangement and really allow us to sonically fulfil our potential.'

Recording started at the Motor Museum Studios in Liverpool before the album was finished off at Livingston Studios in London. Motor Museum is run by Orchestral Manoeuvres in the Dark singer Andy McCluskey, the man behind eighties hits like 'Enola Gay' and 'Joan of Arc'. In fact the drum machine used on the intro to 'Enola Gay' is lying around in the studios – the sheer density of eighties vibes available at the Motor Museum must have been a good omen for a band like The 1975, particularly knowing that OMD had contributed to many of those John Hughes' soundtracks that Healy so often cites as an influence. 'We did a week of pre-production, during which we mainly discussed the aesthetics of the album and listened to lots of records together to get a sense of where we could go with each track,' producer Crossey later explained to *Sound on Sound* magazine. 'Their tracks cross quite a few different styles, so it was really important to make sure that the production had a strong sense of character, a fingerprint that would help define the music as immediately identifiable. One of the things that the band was really clear on was that they wanted to make an album with a colourful, widescreen sound, which had many contrasts in it. They are very much into the soundtracks to 1980s films, as well as Michael Jackson, and this was reflected in the sound image that we were going for. We were not trying to make something that was lo-fi!'

For a bedroom band like The 1975, working in a real studio was a revelation: 'Mike had access to a kind of Disneyland in regards to recording music, and a knowledge and technical understanding that really, really catalysed the creative process,' Healy told music writer Andy McCall. 'If you have such a solid foundation with these techniques of how to record, you really have free rein to be as creative as possible, you're not harboured by anything. I think that's what defined the album essentially.'

The line that Crossey and the band had to negotiate was one of highlighting their pop sensibilities without alienating fans enthralled by the more avant-garde aspects of their music. 'They wanted an impressive pop element to the music, especially in the vocals, and we were pretty unashamed about wanting a song like "Chocolate" to be a smash hit,' Crossey later admitted to journalist Mike Tingen. 'But at the same time we wanted things to be funky and a bit leftfield. There is a lot of ambient leftfield-type music on their EPs, which the band very capably produced themselves, and that's an important aspect of them. Many people got into them via a more underground route, via digging into the more weird things they also do. We really wanted to incorporate all these elements and strike a good balance.'

Three months after the release of *Facedown*, the band's second EP, *Sex* – with Crossey helping out on two tracks – was released. 'Intro/Set 3' is our introduction to *Sex*, a lyrically bizarre drum-machine and feedback wail that almost acts like the band getting all their avant-garde proclivities out of their system before the songs' 'proper' start. 'Undo' is a slightly more straightforward affair, with Healy's almost indecipherable vocal seemingly guilt-wracked about fooling around with an ex. This is difficult, uneasy listening music – no pop fluff here.

Then it's time for full-on 'Sex'. This song, that many

remember from the band's early gigs, is a simplified version of an already very simple riff (U2's 'I Will Follow' springs to mind). We're in the back of Healy's van and we're not there to admire the upholstery. Whether or not they were aware of it, the band the track invokes even more than U2 is The 1975's Cheshire compatriots and near-neighbours Marion. It shares the same driving urgency and Healy's vocal invokes Marion singer Jaime Harding's desperate yodel. There's barely three minutes of 'Sex' on offer, but it's good stuff. It's a song that would mislead many critics; it's pure indie pop without so much as a whiff of funk or glacial ambience. 'We went through so many times of recording that song, to try to get to it to sound... *cool?*' Healy would later recall. 'The instrumentation of that song is the most straight-up indie out of all of our songs. We actually wanted to drop that song – we wanted to lose "Sex" because we thought it was too rock and we could never be taken seriously. Our manager was like, no, you're crazy, this is one of your biggest songs... He was right. Which was annoying.'

'When "Sex" came out,' Healy later told *musicOMH*, 'that was a massive deal for me. So many people told me of how it was "their song" and how they found so much of themselves in the lyrics. I think our songs are so personal to me lyrically – so specific – that people can kind of find themselves in there, you know what I mean? What I have realised is that the human connection that you speak of, that's the most important thing. You can spend months working on the sonics and sound of a record or a track, but if it doesn't have that immediacy of emotion, if it doesn't take you somewhere personally, what's the point?'

'You' seemingly rounds off the EP, Hann's guitars to the fore in a song that has a far more decipherable indie format, with a U2/Big Country influence apparent in its big bass drums and cyclical riffs. This is fairly straightforward, skinny jeans rock and sounds like another band when compared to tracks one and three. Then, after a hefty slice of silence, comes hidden track 'Milk'. Another Foalsesque, straight-ahead rocker whose aggression is nicely undermined by Healy's fey vocal – it would go on to become a fan favourite among the band's early songs.

A video was released to accompany the lead track – a simple black-and-white affair that saw the band playing in their rehearsal room/shed surrounded by pictures of their musical and physical touchstones and influences: Blur, Talking Heads, Marilyn Monroe, Whitney Houston, Michael Jackson, and Eurythmics.

Reviewers felt they could sense other influences too – everyone from My Bloody Valentine to Sigur Rós was cited – and it's that seemingly schizophrenic aspect of the EP that seemed to rile some people and intrigue others. 'It is as if two different bands have got together to do a split single, which is a little off-putting,' offered *Contactmusic*. 'Where The 1975 have written some very strong songs, the schizophrenic nature of this EP is a little confusing and you get a feeling that if they just chose one style to zero in on and master, they could become something very special indeed.'

Website *Glasgowmusic* were clearly enamoured by the lead track but couldn't resist a reference to their near neighbours, Joy Division: 'Manchester four-piece The 1975 are quite clearly not interested in longwinded gentle foreplay and the whispering of sweet nothings in the hope that they might be in store for a twelve-hour tantric love-making session; they would much prefer to proceed directly to the tearing off of knickers for a three-and-a-half minute amphetamine-fuelled dirty fuck. Thrashing guitars, pounding bass and pummelling drums are infiltrated by a dose of synth-enhanced electronica to filthy effect by a band whose members' own conception doesn't predate 1990. If "Love Will Tear Us Apart" then "Sex" Will Keep Us Together.'

No doubts at all though from the *Hit The Floor* site: 'Every track on this is incredible and shows off the band's spectrum of talents with ease and simplicity. We here at *HTF* cannot wait to hear more from this band as they continue to get better and better. If the album release is anything like this, the world will soon know the name of The 1975... and that world will be a better place.'

Music bloggers and niche sites were definitely taking notice of The 1975, but the 'mainstream' media had yet to catch up. In late November 2013 the band got a small write-up in the *Daily Star*, mainly notable for allowing Healy to claim they were holding back on their debut album because he wanted it to be as good as Michael Jackson's *Thriller*.

They'd get some slightly more serious coverage with a piece

in the *Guardian* just prior to The 1975's gig at Sound Control. As part of a series called 'New Band Up North', The 1975 were highlighted as ones to watch by journalist Emily Brinnand: 'I stumbled across them when they were played on Amazing Radio, an independent radio station based in Newcastle. They're a DAB station so they obviously play all over the world and they play new and emerging music. They're very hot on new acts – even before the BBC – always going to gigs, and they're all music lovers themselves at Amazing. I heard "Sex" when it came out and I was like, "This is going to be massive." I got addicted to the song and would obsess over it. It's one of the songs you hear and [sharp intake of breath], you know what I mean? For some reason I just thought, it's going to blow, it's going to explode.'

Brinnand organised an interview with Healy directly – no PR or managers involved at this stage – and realised straight away that the singer wasn't the usual monosyllabic, moochy Manc band member. Healy had his narrative ready – even his story about how the band's name came about was already a highly polished anecdote. 'I could tell he was very conscious of the way he wanted to be perceived and the way he wanted to show off The 1975, like it was his baby,' Brinnand told me. 'How he came up with the band, how they worked through school to make it what it is. He had very romantic ideas about The 1975 and I think that continues with him as frontman of the band. Writing out his answers to my questions it struck me how considered everything was to do with the band. I think that was very much thought out from the beginning and he wanted to kinda flirt with his audience at an early age. Because that's what he was trying to say about love and the youth and sex – they're all themes that he wants that band to be associated with.'

The stage was set for their showcase at Sound Control just two days after the piece appeared. Although he didn't know it, Matthew Healy's life – and the lives of his fellow band members – was about to change beyond all recognition.

FIVE

CHAOS

If you're looking for Sound Control – this key location in the development of The 1975 – you'll find it tucked in between The Thirsty Scholar and Revolution bar in the shadow of Oxford Road train station in Manchester.

Because this is where, as a band, The 1975 took off and took flight – and this pivotal moment took place at a venue already steeped in Manchester music history: 'It used to be a music shop called A1,' explains Ben Taylor, Sound Control's events manager for seven years, now running his own management company, B33. 'Many Manchester musicians bought their gear there. Noel Gallagher bought his guitar there, Reni [Stone Roses] bought his drum kit. We still had people coming in to ask if we could repair their amps for years afterwards.'

'It's spread over three floors, and each floor has its own

character. There's a 150-capacity live room; the basement has a 300-capacity room – more of a warehouse, industrial feel. There's a 450-capacity room in the loft. You get bands in the big room about to head out on tour who do warm-up shows there. We never pigeonholed genres. Steve Harley [of seventies band Cockney Rebel] played there; we've had the Scissor Sisters. Rita Ora did her first-ever live show there.'

Matthew Healy would often make reference to the Sound Control gig at the end of 2012 as a kind of line in the sand, the point at which The 1975's story truly started. He'd sometimes mention it as the band's gigs and their audiences got bigger and bigger: look how far we've come… *it's only a matter of months/years since we were playing Sound Control.*

The Sound Control gig for Wednesday, 5 December had been booked five months earlier, but with a bit of press and some airplay, the word on The 1975 was out. It was all set to be a very different affair to the usual gig in front of a few dozen relatives and mates – this one was a sell-out.

Events manager Ben Taylor remembers the show well – especially the band's friendly attitude towards both the venue and support act Catfish and the Bottlemen: 'They arrived bang on time, no problems. They shared their gear with the other support bands – drums and amps. The crowd was dead mixed. It was maybe even tipping towards more girls. The girls liked 'em! There was a ton of girls at the front. They're not an indie, laddish band.'

Taylor also remembers their request for the lottery scratchcards as part of their rider: 'That's genius. After the catering – 100 quid – they would have come away with five or six quid a head from the gig. The scratchcards are a great idea. If you do that at every show, at some point you're going to win something, right?'

DJ Dan Deighan – who by now had been following the band's fortunes for five years – was also there: 'It was quite a special gig. Seven quid a ticket, Catfish and the Bottlemen as support. About 150 people there. Their first-ever sell-out gig. They were well on the cusp. I remember there were Christmas presents hanging from the ceiling because it was December.'

Audience member Charlie Watts was typical of the kind of young fan there that night. Like many of The 1975's early fan base, he was from the south Manchester/Cheshire borders. He'd been given a USB stick of songs by Drive Like I Do by a friend of the band: 'Chocolate', 'Robbers' and 'Ghosts'.

Watts had been told that Drive Like I Do and The 1975 were one and the same. 'I went along with my sister,' he told me. 'And I went expecting hardly anyone to be there, but it was *rammed*. They had a support act on, Catfish and the Bottlemen, but we didn't really pay attention to them. It wasn't a stage as such, just stands and speakers. The lads came out and set up their own gear, as you do when you're at that level – you do your own soundchecking. They had their hoods up and everything. They only played about seven songs, they only played for half an hour. But it was great. I related to them 'cos they were my age – and the people who were going to see them were my age too. The songs were really relevant – going out, taking something you shouldn't, having a fight with the girlfriend. You'd listen to them and think, *Yeah, I can relate to that.*'

Ben Taylor remembers the atmosphere in the tiny venue: 'It was *chaos*. The first gig I'd ever put in that room and people were crowd surfing and going mad. We thought, *This is nuts.* We were grinning from ear to ear. The band were freaking out to see how much people were enjoying it. They weren't being all cool – you could tell it meant something to them.'

'That was really important for us,' Healy later said, when asked about the gig for the *Psychedelia* video channel. 'There were kids hanging off the ceiling, standing on the bar, trying to get even a glimpse of the show. So that was very memorable for us. It was amazing.'

Emily Brinnand, who'd written the *Guardian* piece about The 1975 which had appeared a few days earlier, was also there: 'I go to a lot of gigs by new bands in Manchester and there's normally about ten people there – they may be good but they're not totally comfortable yet with their set, they may never have played before in front of a crowd. But with these guys, The 1975, it was different. I know you're probably thinking, *You're saying that now that they're huge and play stadiums.* But it was packed… sweaty. They were really tight with their set. And the energy in there was electric, to use a cliché. But you *did* feel the energy, you did feel it was something different. You go to see bands and think: *This is good, I know they're great and have the potential, but they've got a long way to go.* Whereas these guys, I thought… *Your next venue is going to be a lot bigger than Sound Control!'*

Audience member Charlie Watts told me: 'After the gig I went up to Matty. I was like, "Why didn't you play 'Ghosts' tonight? It's a really good song as well." So he said, "It's going to be on the album…" which it never was. That song's never been played at any other gig I've seen and it's never been on any album. So they must have just scrapped it.'

After the gig, the band returned to their dressing room. 'I got them a bottle of champagne on ice,' remembers Taylor. 'The dressing room is up in the loft and after the gig they came upstairs and they were all jumping around. And I passed it to the drummer [George Daniel]. They said, "Who's this for?" I told them, "It's for you, well done!" They couldn't believe it. The drummer had blood all over his hands because he'd really been digging in.'

Dan Deighan: 'When they got the champagne they threw the glasses on the floor and necked it from the bottle. They were pumped up about it.'

Ben Taylor: 'It's in my top ten of shows that I've ever put on. It was their first Manchester sold-out show. It was a buzz. They tweeted a picture that someone had taken – it said "Best Gig Ever".'

After the Sound Control gig, the band headed for London, making their debut in the capital at The Barfly in Camden. It was only supposed to be a short tour – but the band essentially didn't come home for two years as events and demand overtook them. 'The first headline gigs we had were our first headlining tour in December [2013],' Healy later told *FaceCulture*. 'We thought, *this is a really big deal*. Once we started that tour… one thing we have that a lot of other bands don't have is genuine history and genuine playing ability with each other. When we started playing these shows there was an amazing juxtaposition, from it being totally fresh and new but also nostalgic. Because it was the same four friends who'd been playing for ten years. It felt like a genuinely real moment where people were experiencing it for the first time, but for us it had been such a long time coming, we were so prepared for it.'

Some of the shows were still free but word of mouth was spreading and venues were starting to get packed. Reviewers were picking up on the band, though some seemed slightly baffled: 'This Manchester foursome have settled on an unlikely blend of recent indie rock and 1980s white pop-funk,' wrote music journalist Dave Simpson in January 2013, in his review of the band's gig at Soyo in Sheffield for the *Guardian*. It's an amusing review that rather eerily predicts almost exactly what would happen to the band. Simpson is a highly experienced music writer, but it's almost as if he'd gone back to the future, seen how things panned out for The 1975, come back and penned his piece accordingly. 'At least a third of their songs are ridiculously catchy, although it takes some getting over the shock of a sound that puts together Foals/Vampire Weekend-type jerkiness with the middle of the road pop-rock of Deacon Blue.'

Of the frontman, Simpson wrote, 'Healy, who is forever either running a hand through or shaking his outgrown mohawk hairstyle, is a messianic type with a touch of the Johnny Borrell [Razorlight] about him. He is playing a free gig in a packed bar, yet in his mind seems to be living out a stadium rock-type fantasy. When a girl shouts, "Get yer top off!" he heckles her back: "Imagine how misogynistic that would be if I said the same to you." Cringe-factors and the Simple Minds drum-plod of "The City" aside, the instantly singable "Sex", with its simple, sublime guitar motif, do enough to suggest they'll be heard everywhere this year. Healy ends the gig atop the drum kit, thanking the pub audience, section by section, as if he's playing Wembley; The 1975 may be a band who are loathed as well as loved.'

Meanwhile, back in Manchester, Ben Taylor was keen to get the band to pay a return visit to Sound Control after the wild success of the December gig. Even after a matter of weeks, things had changed: 'My promoter instincts kicked in after the gig and I said it would be great to get you to play upstairs in the larger room. Soon after I got an email… Sorry, the next show in Manchester has already been booked. That's when [promoters] SJM came in. The next Manchester show was at The Deaf Institute [in February 2013]. Catfish supported them again. I went. After that it went boom. They had a plan. They knew. And it worked. They had a bigger team around them as The 1975.'

Charlie Watts, who'd seen the band at Sound Control

just a few months earlier, noticed a big change at their next Manchester show: 'From Sound Control to The Deaf Institute, it was different,' he told me. 'When I went to The Deaf Institute, 70 per cent of the crowd were singing the songs back. Bearing in mind half these songs hadn't been online, there was no album, so they had a lot more… *crazy* fans: people stalking them, hunting them down for the tracks. Matthew made a remark to the crowd along the lines of, "How do you know all the words?" The Deaf Institute was a fantastic gig, as opposed to the Sound Control gig; they played a full set and that would pretty much be the album that they'd later release.'

'We were playing clubs to 200 kids, where 100 of them would wait afterwards to meet us, with fucking neck tattoos,' Healy recalled to *SPIN* magazine. 'The first bit of our fandom was hardcore.'

In a rare example of him getting a word in edgeways bass player Ross MacDonald told the BBC, 'We'd spent so long prior to releasing any music just doing it for ourselves and working ourselves out a little bit. When we booked our first headline tour – we'd never really done a headline show of our own before – that was *new*. Then as the EPs came out the interest grew, we were baffled how we were selling out shows.'

The week after The Deaf Institute gig, the band released a video for 'Chocolate' prior to its release in March 2013 as the lead track of their new EP. It saw the band driving around in the rain in a 1970s Ford Consul – tellingly, it was George and Matthew who were sitting up front in the car; Adam Hann and

Ross MacDonald were in the back seat. Healy got the chance to take his top off, smoke a lot and snog a model, too. 'They are really nice guys,' video director Gareth Phillips recalled to journalist Joanna Longawa. 'When we made "Chocolate", The 1975 were just starting to blow up. I really wanted the band to feel comfortable and natural, and be themselves… I didn't want any acting or over-the-top performance. The song is about smoking weed, so we needed Matthew to be puffing all day. The poor guy had to smoke constantly; of course it was just tobacco. He was looking green and sickly by the end of the day but this added to the realistic performance. He looked great on camera, he's got real charisma. The model was sourced by the band; it wasn't difficult to get her and Matthew to act intimately. She did a great job. I didn't really need to give them much direction.'

'Chocolate' would later be voted the best song played on Radio 1 over the last five years in an online listeners' poll, beating the likes of Bastille and Fall Out Boy. But for now, the song – one of their oldest – was simply the lead track from the band's third EP, *Music For Cars*, perhaps a nod to (one of) their old band names. It starts with 'Anobrain', a typically breathy scene setter in Japan/Talk Talk/ Scritti Politti territory. It's there to get us ready for lead track 'Chocolate', with Healy in full-on strangulated cockney mode as he sings about the joys of smoking weed and ducking and diving the boys in blue. It's a strange song inasmuch as it has three uber-catchy choruses as well as an Afrobeat vibe that echoes that great lost track 'Ghosts'.

Third track 'HNSCC' again gives us an icy instrumental break, its towering blips and drones like a lost section from a Christopher Nolan soundtrack. It's a technique that would be replicated later on the band's second album, with glacial instrumentals acting as dividers between upbeat and slowdown tracks. The Drive Like I Do theme is continued with 'Head.Cars. Bending', a bowel-shifting bass-led chill out, which seems to be a tale of jealousy. The circumstances of the track's creation were unusual, to say the least. The band were in the middle of recording the EP when Healy got news that his grandmother was gravely ill. He'd gone to her bedside when the end was near. Healy was by now channelling every aspect of his life into the band's music. Some were joyous, others tragic: 'It was like a diary – something would happen to me and we would write about it,' he later told BBC Radio 1. 'My nanna died when we were doing *Music For Cars*. She died right in the middle of it. I was devastated by that. One night we were working on that record and I was just playing the guitar through the laptop. I played for about twenty minutes. That became the fourth track on the EP without me even realising it was being recorded. I think those moments stand out in our body of work. We're a pop band, we love things that rely on classic pop sensibilities. But there's a genuine strain of honesty and humanity and real life running through all of it.'

Music For Cars ends with 'Me'. Has there ever been a more Healyesque song title? It's 4am and the party is over. Healy abandons his usual yelp and croons us to sleep with a backdrop of wooden clicks, finger snaps, bass booms and drones. There's even a taste of that most eighties of devices, a sax break straight out of *Pretty in Pink*, to round things off – an outrageous move for a young band in 2013. Healy's increasing interest in the instrument would bring saxophonist and childhood friend John Waugh into the fold – he would join the band as a touring member, bringing them back up to a five-piece unit, as in their Drive Like I Do days.

Reviewers – on the whole – were coming round to the band, particularly their habit of mixing pop hooks with obscure electro noodling. '"Chocolate" positively hogs the spotlight,' offered *Pop Matters*. 'It ends up feeling like the odd one out in this context: the electronic overtones feel like a better suit for the band overall and end up being the reason why you'd want to hear more from this band. Regardless of whether you think the heart of *Music for Cars* is in its breakout star or in the electronic mood pieces surrounding it, The 1975's third EP is also the one that really signals they're here.

'The first two EPs had promise, but the five songs here fulfil it: it feels like it's here that The 1975 finally show their cards and give the listener a reason to start paying attention to them. Whether they'll continue on this upwards trajectory remains to be seen, but what's certain is that *Music for Cars* is an interesting and most importantly a very good set of songs.'

Even the Americans were starting to sit up and take notice: 'Although the name The 1975 might imply overwhelming nostalgia, these Manchester rockers aren't just focused on the past,' said *Rolling Stone*. 'On their new EP *Music for Cars*, The 1975 wrap two pop anthems inside a trio of hazy, atmospheric journeys. "Chocolate" is a blissful track with a noodling guitar lead and unhurried stadium-sized drums, while "Head.Cars. Bending" lurches ahead with synth claps, clattering syncopation and angelic vocal harmonies. "Anobrain", "HNSCC" and "Me", meanwhile, slip in between with hypnotic ambience and ethereal voices.'

But not everyone was so keen. The *NME* – a paper the band would have a long-term up-and-down relationship with over the next few years – were clear in their opinion and their advice: 'Where have Fall Out Boy been during their three-year hiatus? Because it sounds like they've been passing tips to Manchester four-piece The 1975. Despite its gangster storyline this is like the Illinois emos on a Thomas Cook package holiday, all glossy production and cheery tropical guitar licks. Avoid.'

The *NME*'s advice was clearly not taken. Boosted by airplay that shifted the band from night-time to daytime, 'Chocolate' became a Top 20 hit. 'That's when things first got *really* big,' Healy later told *Clash* magazine. 'And it was weird because you imagine everything coming together like that, but you've no idea it's actually going to happen. We went on tour with Two Door Cinema Club straight away, and then went to America, so I only heard it [the single] about twice. It was crazy when we got back to the UK though, because that song goes back a long way. I sit there and think, *Wow, those words came out of my head*.'

To capitalise on the song's success, a re-recorded version of 'The City' – with extra boom boom pow courtesy of Mike Crossey – was released in April. Another hit. 'It's a very humbling experience, you know, that people are embracing what we do,' Healy told *Some Kind of Awesome*, as it was clear the song was going to be the one that would push them overground. 'We didn't have any aspirations for it being accepted by the mainstream media in the way that it has been. So, I think it's kind of been like a catalyst in the progression of the understanding of ourselves really, and the understanding of the band, cause we've never had an emotional response. We've never really gone through any sort of process of qualification or validation as a band.'

Video director Tim Mattia – whose credits include working with everyone from Marilyn Manson to Nicole Scherzinger – was brought in to give the band a black-and-white sheen for the promo to accompany 'The City'. The video set out the band's stall in terms of image: moodiness, tattoos, cityscapes, neon lights, sex and models smoking fags. Mattia would work repeatedly with the band, producing some of their best videos.

The original plan had been to make three EPs, then release an album. But with a small window of time available, they decided to knock out a fourth. 'Our manager rang me and said, "We've got to do another EP",' Healy would later recall to Radio 1's Huw Stephens. 'I said, "We can't, it doesn't work like that. We can't just do another one." Then we realised… Why not? You've got a week, make a record in a week.'

The band's final EP – called *IV* in an echo of Peter Gabriel and the way his albums were known numerically – was released in May 2013 and started with the new version of 'The City', with all that added drum power provided by producer Mike Crossey. It also sported a more throbby, disorientating bass line – it feels far more like a hit than the earlier attempt but maintains that small-town Wilmslow longing for a more exciting life – perhaps, temptingly, it exists just down the M56, just out of reach, yet achievable. 'Haunt//Bed' is a beautiful track, with Healy replying to his own multi-tracked vocal over layer after layer of synths, guitars and a simple four four beat. It uses a similar vibe to some of the band's instrumentals, but this is more than a mere bridging track; it's a lovely song in its own right. 'So Far (It's Alright)' has one of those distinctive, three-note noodly riffs from Hann, with Healy's vocal sounding almost Ed Sheeran-like in the way his words scat and trip around the beat of the track. 'Fallingforyou' has Healy's flat Cheshire vowels coming out (his pronunciation of 'home' is very Wilmslow) as he professes his love at some ungodly hour of the morning over a Yazooesque synth backing. The drum machines are pure 'In the Air Tonight' era Phil Collins, echoing Healy's beloved *Face Value* LP by the former Genesis drummer turned eighties solo star.

There's a sense here of this final EP being leaner and less ambient – song after song hits home without the need for an instrumental breather. It's like they really meant business this time around. 'I think the best EP we did was *IV*,' Healy later told the BBC. 'We made each of those records [the EPs] in a week – wrote them, recorded them – and they were all done in my bedroom. No one knew who I was – it's so nice to think about that time – nobody questioned me, nobody wanted me to fail, nobody wanted us to do anything apart from exist. We were making really, really honest records then. *IV* is probably my favourite record.'

The EPs also put the band in a very strong bargaining position when they signed marketing and distribution deals. They brought a fan base to the table thanks to these releases, giving them the upper hand in terms of their deal – essentially a licensing agreement with Polydor, Interscope and Universal. While they might not wish to be labelled 'indie' band, the reality is, The 1975 approached the release of their debut album with a genuine sense of independence: 'A big glamorous pop band like us has become a band of the people,' Healy explained later to *Radio.com*. 'And all of the cooler bands that are doing things slightly less pop, more theatrical, are more controlled by the industry. It's kind of a weird irony.'

The 1975 were now on the brink of something special – creatively and commercially. The short, sweet review of *IV* in the *Daily Star* summed things up: 'After breaking through with "Chocolate", the Mancs should match Bastille for successful rock thanks to an EP full of easily hummable hooks. The way Matthew Healy sings "Best job he ever 'ad" on lead tune "The City" is wonderfully silly. The 1975 are the sound of 2013.'

In amongst this flurry of recorded output, the band had

managed a quick jaunt to America to play the SXSW music and media festival in March. It turned out to be an eventful experience: 'We were renting a house off some baseball star who was really religious,' Daniel would later tell MTV. 'And his mum turned up and found lots of, like, paraphernalia, and found out we'd been sharing a bed – three guys – and they called us "Godless animals" and they chased us out of the house with a gun! They didn't like it! I was like, Come on! I thought we were in Austin! I didn't think this was, like, *hick* territory. They hated us.'

That three-in-a-bed sleep might well have been one of the last decent rests the band would have for a while: 'We played about eleven shows in five days at SXSW, then headed up to Milwaukee and played up there,' Healy explained to *Scenewave*. 'Then went to Chicago, and up to Ohio. We didn't really go to bed the entire time, to be honest – the whole thing is a complete blur. It's our first time we've ever been there, and to have all these people at our shows was amazing. We had this realisation that we'd sort of travelled from my bedroom to America and all these people are watching us and that was awesome. Eleven shows in five days! I mean if we weren't going out, we were onstage, it was huge.'

These weren't the biggest venues in the world – 100-plus people in some cases – but they were selling out. Meanwhile, interest in the band was growing back home, thanks to the EPs. 'Every single show seemed to surprise us at that point, because we didn't really know what was going on, especially because we were out of the country,' Ross MacDonald would later recall in an interview with Radio 1. 'We had no idea the fan base was building as much as it was while we were away. You're so isolated from that kind of thing when you're in a tour bus, you never really get to grips with what's going on in the real world.'

The band would return to the US in the summer for their first proper tour, playing support to Californian rock band The Neighbourhood. 'We wanted to do something with these guys but I thought it was going to be a reach,' The Neighbourhood's Jesse Rutherford explained to video channel *When The Gramophone Rings*. 'We are at very similar point in our careers. Thankfully, these guys wanted to do it. They're not on tour with us because our music styles are the same – if anything they're pretty damned different – but our visions are very similar. And that's what feels good – to be in a room with a bunch of people who have a similar mindset is a good feeling, it's a vibe.'

Healy was asked about what was next for them. His detailed explanation of the band's massively expanded itinerary is as revealing as it is jaw-dropping: 'We fly home tomorrow. Land at 6am, UK time. Play Glastonbury that same day. Go to sleep. Play Glastonbury again on The Other Stage the next day. Leave that night, get up at five in the morning, fly to Rome, come back; then do five gigs in France, go home, then fly out to Los Angeles to shoot a video for our next single in four days. We then come home, play three festivals, fly back to Los Angeles, do a run of five shows, fly back to the UK as a transfer to fly to Japan, then we're in Japan for ten days… It's so ludicrous.'

Though Healy was a regular visitor to Reading and Leeds as a music fan, 2013 marked The 1975's debut as performers at Glastonbury. 'We got to the side of the stage about five minutes before we went on so it was a pretty intense day, but the crowd were amazing,' Healy remembered in an interview with *FaceCulture*. 'There were thousands of people there. I didn't realise how big The Other Stage was – it's like the size of the Reading main stage. I'm just lost at the moment and can't believe that all of this is kicking off.'

'Please dance with us,' Healy told the Glastonbury crowd as they broke into 'Chocolate'. 'Otherwise we'll look ridiculous.'

Another thing that seemed to be getting ridiculous was the sheer scope of the band's ambition. Emboldened by their performance, The 1975 decided that by 2016, they'd be headlining at Glastonbury – not The Other Stage but The Pyramid Stage. 'Why not be one of the greats?' Healy said, as if offended by anyone doubting his plan. 'There's no point in us stopping now, we want to be one of the biggest bands in the world. One of the biggest bands of all time. That's not our delusion. People have started embracing this music.'

Healy had some other important dates in his diary for July 2013 – and unfortunately for him, the dates clashed. His mum Denise had announced she was getting married to her boyfriend, Lincoln Townley, in Portugal. The date was set. Then The 1975 got an offer they couldn't refuse: 'I was just in

Philadelphia with a ridiculous hangover, asleep in the back of a car,' Healy told *The Chronicle* in his parents' native northeast. 'One of the guys from our management called up and said The Stones had asked if we had any time… that's how he worded it, but I'm pretty sure it wasn't Keith or Mick ringing up to see if we were free! It was one of those moments when you take a step back and think the whole thing has just got bigger than we ever thought.'

Anything connected with Denise Welch is immediately fair game for the British press – the wedding was thought to be the subject of a big money deal with a glossy magazine – and the tabloids immediately seized on the news of Healy's non-appearance in favour of playing with The Rolling Stones as a 'snub' to his mum's nuptials. Welch went into Twitter overdrive to set the record straight. Referring to her 'two amazing sons, Matt and Louis,' she sent a series of tweets to limit any damage it might cause: 'I could not be more proud of them both and I love them with all my heart. They have seen some quite dramatic changes in their lives over the last few years… they have dealt with these changes incredibly well. Louis and my husband-to-be Lincoln have forged a great friendship, something I'm so happy about. Matt is constantly touring with his band The 1975 and, after years of hard work, it's paying off. The downside to that is that he cannot make it to our wedding on Saturday as the band are supporting The Rolling Stones in Hyde Park and was specially requested by Mick Jagger.'

So, as his mum got married in the Algarve watched by Christopher Biggins and The Krankies, Matthew was at Hyde Park with The Stones. The venerable rockers hadn't played Hyde Park for forty-four years, since their legendary free gig after the death of guitarist Brian Jones. This time, the gig very definitely wasn't free – some fans had paid a lot of money to see Mick Jagger and Co and clearly didn't take too kindly to the likes of The 1975 and their electronic posturing. One audience member in particular was heckling them from the start – they pressed on but it was clearly a distraction. But Matthew Healy had learned how to deal with people like that on the pub floor of The Phoenix in Manchester and knew what to do. 'I know you hate us, mate,' he told the heckler, 'but we're supporting The Stones, not you!' The band then fittingly went into 'Settle Down'.

Healy explained his feelings about the day to *Harper's Bazaar* – if nothing else, when you've supported The Stones, you get asked questions by a better class of publication: 'You've got 50,000 people there – which I don't mind too much, because I quite like the idea of a singular identity crowd, moving and reacting as one – but when you've got a Rolling Stones' crowd, the first 7,000 are hardcore Stones' fans who've been to almost every single tour, it's the hottest day of the year and they don't want to see some jumped-up kids playing their nu-school R&B inspired pop music.'

Aside from dealing with hecklers with aplomb, Healy had another reason to believe he and the band had the last laugh that day: as they tore into 'Chocolate', Jagger himself was spotted at the side of the stage, dancing and singing along. 'It was a good day,' Healy concluded. 'It was one of those bucket list moments.'

After Hyde Park, the band headed back to America – via Belgium and Germany – to do a string of California dates, including the legendary Troubadour club in Hollywood, the launching pad for everyone from the Eagles to Mötley Crüe. The 1975 received a considerable boost before the opening night of the mini-tour by appearing on the Conan O'Brien show, performing 'Chocolate'. 'We had one of those moments where we thought, we shouldn't be doing this, why are we here? This is all too much,' said Healy in an interview backstage at the Troubadour with Robert Herrera. 'I think it's a representation of just how far we've come.'

'The 1975 played their first show in Los Angeles and might have put their own notch on the historic walls of the fifty-six-year-old Troubadour,' said a review of the show on local music website *Killing The Cabinet*. 'Only time will tell, but the Manchester group was almost flawless... delivering a very rehearsed set which had everyone's attention. The last three songs of the night, "Chocolate", "Sex" and "You", took the crowd's expectations from "met" to "exceeded". These guys are on their way to very big things. They've moved into our top three best bands of 2013 and might grab the crown when the year's all over.'

After finishing up in San Diego and mopping up a few

more UK festival dates, it was time for another slice of culture shock for the band with the first of many visits to Japan. 'When we got here there were girls waiting for us at the airport with chocolates they'd made with our faces on,' Healy would later tell *Clash* magazine about their trip to Tokyo. 'To come to the other side of the world, to a place you've never been anywhere near, and have people know your songs is really humbling. It's crazy how an idea can start in a room and spread across the world.'

With the new album just weeks away, a new version of 'Sex' was released with a new video. British director Adam Powell was in charge this time around; filming had taken place in Los Angeles, squeezed around their Hyde Park commitments with The Rolling Stones. Powell had previously worked with Birdy and Example and was someone who would collaborate with the band several times over the coming years. 'The video is about what the song's about, I suppose,' Healy told *FaceCulture*, just before the shoot. 'It's about being beautiful, but not necessarily living the most beautiful existence.'

The usual total black-and-white aesthetic was largely abandoned in favour of full colour, lots of sex and lots of drugs. It was a signifier – *now that the EPs were done, the album is going to be different so don't expect more of the same.* 'We really love the dualism in the video between the muted almost black-and-white performance shots of the band set against the cinematic colour of the narrative,' Healy told *Some Kind of Awesome*. 'We have used black and white for every other video to date, so it seemed like incorporating colour would be a massive step for us to make; in reality the creative decision made itself as we liked the obvious separation that the colour provided for the narrative against the performance parts of the video.'

He went on to explain that the band's album and EPs were totally separate entities: 'Each EP is like a polaroid of a specific time and place, in regards to the visuals of the album, we want to make short films for our videos – like trailers almost, in the same way our songs are the narrative to our formative years the videos are the narrative to those songs. As a video "Sex" feels very uncompromised, unpredictable and from an artistic viewpoint, very honest. That is always our main goal as a band. We are very proud of it. We found a true collaborative spirit with Adam Powell the director. It was our desire to work with him and his passion and understanding towards our vision that led us to shooting in LA.'

There was of course that schedule: gig after gig, festival after festival. But playing at Reading and Leeds that August of 2013 must surely have been a highlight. They'd been here before: 'Leeds and Reading hold a special place in our hearts,' Ross MacDonald later told the BBC: 'We went in 2007 – me, Matthew and George all shared a two-man tent. That was the first festival we'd been to. We said, one day we're going to play this festival. And we did it. It was a real tearjerker that moment. We played "Chocolate" and the whole place erupted. It put in our minds how far we'd come.'

In 2013, the band put in a series of bravura performances

– including a set in Leeds where Healy climbed the rigging tower and filmed the audience with his phone. Catfish and the Bottlemen were also on the bill of the dual festival that year, but so too were another band with whom Healy had history: Green Day. It would have been just over ten years since young Matthew Healy had been dragged up onstage to play bass with the American band. Now he was playing the same festival bill as them as The 1975 were hailed as the hottest band in Britain and the potential 'saviours of guitar music', a tag they'd picked up after the guitar-heavy indie stomp of 'Sex' seemed to wrong-foot some music writers. 'I don't really listen,' Healy told MTV. 'Calling us a guitar band – you might as well call us a drum band. The guitars are merely a detail really. We just have a post-modern outlook on everything we do and our music represents that mentality.'

Healy was, as ever, talking an excellent fight. But if the forthcoming album's contents – not to mention its sales – didn't match up to the singer's bravura, then it was a long way for them to fall. Healy seemed to be bracing himself. 'Once I've made a record and it's the statement that I wanna make and it looks and it smells the way that I want it to do, that's all I can do,' he told *The Edge*. 'Music and art is so subjective and that's what's amazing about it, and that's what can make and break artists. That is an album written way before anybody knew us, so I feel that my only creative responsibility is to just make whatever I do as good as possible. I can't do anything else.'

SIX

AN ODE TO CASSETTE TAPES AND MICHAEL JACKSON

The 1975 – Healy in particular – had spent a lot of time talking up their debut album. 'We're a closed band and we haven't been listening to any contemporary music because it would make too much of an impact on our sound,' he told the *Daily Star*. 'We want the album to be a proper debut that is culturally defining, as good as Michael Jackson's *Thriller*, so we've held back the big singles until it gets released.'

It was typically ludicrous quotes like this from Healy that would truly endear him to the nation's journalists; used to dealing with processed pop stars who'd been media trained to within an inch of their lives, they were beginning to realise that all you had to do was put a recording device near the singer's mouth and he'd be guaranteed to generate good copy. The *Guardian's* Alexis Petridis would later describe Healy as, 'a man who happily seems to have made it his life's mission to never knowingly think before speaking when in the presence of a journalist'.

Or, in the words of Dean Adams from *Drowned in Sound*, Healy was a 'peacock of a singer [who] says things in interviews that are so ridiculous that it seems the only media training he's ever had involved meeting Noel Gallagher in a lift.'

It was down to quietly spoken guitarist Adam Hann to take a more measured approach on what to expect from the debut album: 'On the EPs there's a lot of elements of shoegaze, of that kind of dreamy pop element and then there's a lot of R&B,' he told *The Rave*. 'With the album the idea of that was to try and almost make a cinematic soundtrack to our lives, so there's quite a lot of eighties pop in there and it's kind of an ode to cassette tapes and Michael Jackson posters and the nineties and stuff like that.'

The band's album was released on download, CD and the newly-fashionable and burgeoning vinyl format on 2 September 2013. Any band worth its salt should have a track named after themselves, and the debut album from The 1975 – called *The 1975* – starts with a track called 'The 1975'. It's a bass buzz, multi-layered scene-setter, the likes of which was found on their early EPs, with its heavily treated vocals promising us a late-night journey we won't forget in a hurry. It doesn't hang around for long before 'The City' leads things off properly. Already such a familiar track from its previous outings, it acts as a powerful calling card for newcomers, as well as a reassuring sense of all being well from the band's existing fan base. 'M.O.N.E.Y' – a possible name check to the Manchester band of the same name – ticks the box of the nineties R&B groove so beloved of Healy, as well as tempting in the casual Ed Sheeran fan with the singer's ability to replicate the scat style of singing that Sheeran was currently conquering the world with. 'It's a song about the fact I find it difficult to have platonic relationships with women and the way I'm constantly in search of the next high,' Healy would explain to *Clash* magazine. 'Those aren't good qualities in anyone but because it's dressed up in major pop music with a real sense of openness people relate to it and give me the benefit of the doubt.'

'Chocolate' is next, with their irresistible drug-loving song from way back in the day proving just as catchy within the context of an album. After the drugs comes, unsurprisingly, 'Sex', and the album is already starting to sound like a greatest-hits compilation. It's getting silly now; we are being battered with an onslaught of weapons-grade rock/funk/pop and we're only a handful of tracks in.

Normal bands would spread out the killer tracks, but The 1975 appear to be in no mood for messing about. 'Talk!' invokes The Police, even with a touch of cod Jamaican à la Sting to add to Healy's already considerable range of accents. 'An Encounter' gives us a quick instrumental breather before the single-finger synth pulse of 'Heart Out' makes you wonder where the hell they've been hiding such an impossibly catchy tune. The intro recalls 'London Loves'-era Blur – then it's

Duran Duran meets Hall & Oates as Healy corrals his band mates into a song that seems to flag up all of their strong points and touchstones in the space of one track. Healy implores his girl to work out just how sensitive and fascinating he is over a soundtrack of time-warped synths, guitars and drums that haven't seen the light of day since Live Aid. It even has a sax solo. It's so eighties, it's like being hit repeatedly over the head with a Molly Ringwald box set by someone wearing leg warmers. As great as it is, the song makes them fair game for any critics who might think the band should really be called The 1985, but by this stage they genuinely don't seem to care – we are halfway through the album and they've delivered a stand-out track.

'Heart Out' shimmers directly into 'Settle Down'; again we are firmly in the eighties and again it's irresistible. Funky Strat guitars and Level 42 bass thwonks make it clear for anyone wondering where its roots really lie. Lyrically, like many tracks on the album – 'Chocolate' in particular – it details small-town life in painstaking detail. Here, the band are talking directly to their constituency about their lives. 'Robbers' is next, the oldest song on offer. Essentially a slowed-down 'Heart Out', it's a Soft Cell/OMD ballad, placed just after the mid-point of the album, just like they used to in the old days. Healy's voice whoops, yelps and cracks in this cinematic track that deserves its place in music history for its use of the world 'chafe' if nothing else.

'Girls' gets us back uptempo with Hann shining, with

his interlocking riff snaking around Healy at his best, again talking direct to their listeners about their lives and how they live them. Like many tracks here, the band use those cascading arpeggio synth runs, so beloved of Duran Duran and their ilk, to underpin another album track that sounds like a single-in-waiting.

A quick instrumental break comes with '12' – we need it to protect us from the onslaught of catchiness – before 'She Way Out'. It starts with a lyrical gag, Healy accidentally forgetting to compare his girl's face to something from a magazine as he did in 'Robbers'. It suffers slightly from being not quite as good as some of the previous tracks, despite being cut from the same cloth, but it's still better than most band's filler material.

'Menswear' wisely takes things back down, with Healy again talking right at his fan base, even referring to himself in the lyrics in a pseudo rap as he tells a tale of drunkenly copping off at a friend's wedding. 'Pressure' is pure Go West circa 'King of Wishful Thinking' – perhaps it's time to re-evaluate the work of Peter Cox and Richard Drummie, because they seem to have directly or indirectly influenced what's on offer here.

Healy waits till the end to break our hearts, though. With 'Is There Someone Who Can Watch You', he directly addresses the break-up of his parents' marriage just as the band took off. His concern is not for them but for his younger brother. 'We finished the album and we realised there was one element missing – a really raw moment,' Healy would explain to *Front Row Live*. 'In the time the band got popular, my parents separated, we sold the family house. I have a little brother and I don't get to see him anymore. So it's a song of me hoping that there's someone to watch my little brother.' Over some almost gospelly piano chords, he frets over his brother and whether he's OK in the aftermath of the split. You can hear his every breath and practically hear his tears on the keyboard – he seems to stop the song early, as if too upset to continue. With that, the song – and the album – are done.

Healy had given the album his all and he couldn't contain his excitement after it was completed: 'We all went on a night out, it was five in the morning and I made the engineer go and steal the keys to the studio,' he remembered to *Musicstage*. 'We went back and broke in so we could listen to the record all the way through – we were so excited about it.'

With all of Healy's big talk you might forgive the critics for taking their chance to put the boot in when *The 1975* was released. They didn't... on the whole. 'The 2013 self-titled debut album from The 1975 is a superb album that finds the Manchester outfit poised on the brink of stardom,' said *AllMusic*. 'When rock guitars meet dance-floor synths, eighties influences become hard to deny, but while The 1975 definitely have a retro vibe (hence the name), the alchemy of how they bring those influences to bear is totally contemporary. While many of the tracks here bring to mind such icons as Peter Gabriel, INXS, and U2, they also fit nicely next to artists of the same moment, like Passion Pit, Temper Trap, and M83. It helps that lead singer/songwriter Matthew Healy has a compelling tenor croon that can soar like Bono one minute and coo like Lionel Richie the next.'

Furthermore, the online music guide said: 'There is also a sophistication to the band's songs, and an instinct to blur genre lines that makes it hard to box them into one easy-to-define sound. In that sense, the band also recalls the way Fall Out Boy combined the rhythmic phrasing and melodies of contemporary R&B with their own brand of driving, guitar-based emo-rock. Much has been made of The 1975's avowed love of eighties John Hughes' movies, and many of the cuts here, like the thrilling, lovesick "Settle Down" and the sparkling "Girls", play with such great narrative momentum that they sound like songs culled from a Hughes soundtrack. Meanwhile, cuts like "The City", "Chocolate", and "Sex" drive and climb like the best anthemic 1980s stadium rock, rolling a host of influences into a single distinct sound that, the moment it hits your ears, becomes timeless.'

For the American market, *Rolling Stone* – a publication that would fall in love with the band after the success of their second album – were rather more sniffy. They gave the album just two stars out of five: 'The 1975 could use some enunciation lessons and an editor,' the review said. 'Their debut is a long, often inscrutable set that rifles through synth-rock references like Neon Trees doing a poor M83 impression. Their would-be smash, "Sex", is LCD Soundsystem's "All My Friends" via The Killers' "Somebody Told Me", but the LP mostly forces unconvincing emo lyrics into a bloopy 1980s package.'

Some reviewers – such as 1980s-obsessed *Independent on Sunday* writer Simon Price – seemed slightly offended by both the album and the band: 'Manchester indie quartet The 1975 formed because they realised that making music was "better than going to work". Sadly, that level of inspired thinking permeates their debut album. With its airbrushed major-key melodies, air-freshener synths and pained vocals, it's reminiscent of contemporary MOR bands such as the Temper Trap and the more vintage flavours of Johnny Hates Jazz. It's a Gary Barlow idea of what indie music sounds like. It'll probably be huge. Ho hum.'

'The critics were very confused about us around the first record', George Daniel recalled in an interview with *SPIN*. 'And they accused us of being confused sometimes… like, *This band doesn't know what they want to be*. We *do*, we just want to be different things, because that's a generational way of creating music… that's the way that we consume it, so that's also the way that we like to create it.'

But what about those people who had watched the band develop and grow over the years? What did they make of The 1975's debut? 'Listen to the album – how many hit songs are on it?' says DJ Dan Deighan, who watched the band morph from Drive Like I Do. 'They write singles. "Girls"? It's a hit! I knew it from the first time I heard it. They write big songs. If you listen to old demos – these songs have been thought out for a long time. Maybe it took eight years to perfect "Chocolate". They've had a long time to get them right.'

Promoter Ben Hiard, who had put on gigs for the band more than five years earlier, said: 'The songs off that first album! You've got "Sex" which is urgent, post punky. Then you've got "Chocolate" – considering it's essentially about drugs, that's unique when you hear it on the radio. "Girls" is an eighties pop banger… Amazing.'

The band's Sound Control gig – played just eight months before the album's release – now seemed like a very long time ago. I asked the man who put the gig on, Ben Taylor, what made them and their debut album so special: 'They looked the part,' he told me. 'There was a swagger about them. People pay more attention when you have that. But the songs are good. You could pick five or six singles off that first record.'

Journalist Emily Brinnand: 'The first album was very poppy, it was always going to please the teenage girls. Very addictive, hooky, I really liked it.'

Despite the mixed reviews from the critics, it became very clear, very quickly that the album was going to do very well indeed. Their nearest competition was the 'comeback' album from Trent Reznor's Nine Inch Nails, *Hesitation Marks*. By midweek, it was apparent that this was a one-horse race: *The 1975* was outselling *Hesitation Marks* two to one. 'It's such a weird thing,' Healy told Radio X when it was officially confirmed they'd gone to No. 1. 'It's rare that I'm lost for words. It's normally difficult to shut me up.'

Unsurprisingly, Healy managed to cobble a few thoughts together for the occasion: 'We can't really express how we feel because it encompasses so many things: how proud we are of ourselves, how proud we are of the fact that a band like us who have been together for ten years with no real agenda, with no real ambition of being accepted on that level... to have a band like that get a No. 1 debut record is a reflection that people still want to invest in genuine music. It's mental.'

He continued: 'I tried to think about what this year's been like and with stuff like that, like supporting The Stones, outselling Trent Reznor and that kind of thing it's like... you know when you have a holiday romance? It's only when you return home you get a real perspective of what it was. We're kind of like on this perpetual holiday romance with no chance to look back and reflect. Those songs, man, when we hear those songs it's just us in my bedroom. It's so difficult to have an objective opinion on how people are perceiving them. It's just mind-blowing.'

Back in Wilmslow, even their old music teacher was celebrating: 'I am delighted with their success,' Wilmslow High head of music Gary Morley told the *Macclesfield Express*. 'Not just with the No. 1 album, but with the positive music press they are receiving and their tour successes. It is great to see they remain genuinely nice lads, very grounded and level-headed. They seem to be really enjoying the ride.'

Healy's mum Denise used her column in the *Birmingham Mail* to shout about their success, despite the potential risk to their street cred. 'I'm the proudest mum in the world,' she wrote. 'My son Matt's band, The 1975, are No. 1 in the UK charts with their debut album. I made a pact with myself that I wouldn't talk too much about the band because they are cool and I am not. However, the four boys started the band when they were fourteen, so this is no overnight success. They have worked so hard over the years, written all their own material and it's paid off. The album is truly amazing and, when I listen to the songs Matt has written, I can't help feeling that we did something right. I'm obviously very proud of their achievements and that I have seen them grow from four stroppy teenagers into the lovely, kind, young men they are today.'

But later, the band would grumble that the magic of their achievement was spoilt by knowing too soon that they'd achieved a No. 1 with their debut. It was, in a sense, too easy: 'It was ruined,' George Daniel later told *Guitar Sessions*. 'It was released on Monday and by Tuesday night, all the people who work with us were saying, "You've got the No. 1 after two days, no one's going to beat you now." We were like, "Come on, you can't say that!" That was Tuesday and we had Wednesday, Thursday, Friday, Saturday and then Sunday when we found out. We had the whole week to come to terms with it.'

Alongside the success in Britain, there was the small matter of the album's US sales. All that touring from the early days of 2013 had clearly paid off: The 1975 entered the *Billboard* chart at No. 28, nestled between Macklemore & Ryan Lewis and Alabama & Friends. All that hard touring graft had paid off.

Back home, excitement about the band built throughout the month of September: they played their first headline slot at the

Hull Freedom Festival: 'That one was really special,' Healy told *Soundsphere* magazine. 'I didn't realise we were headlining and I didn't realise how many people were there. I wear glasses and I don't normally wear them onstage. It doesn't normally matter that much. But halfway through the set I realised how far back the crowd went. It was insane.'

They then did a sold-out show at Shepherd's Bush Empire – remember, they'd played the capital's Barfly just nine months earlier. London reviewers seemed fascinated by the band, their sound, their influences and Healy himself: 'For their hour onstage, The 1975 were odder, more entrancing and more glorious still,' said the *Evening Standard*. 'Even when three of the Cheshire foursome hunched over keyboards which were too small and too low for them, like a mutant, homunculus Kraftwerk, the female half of the sell-out audience screamed as if they were experiencing One Direction. As it was, the band went in all directions, as if randomly selecting influences from a pop tombola. Talking Heads, Doves, Level 42, A Flock of Seagulls, The Thompson Twins and White Lies were there and, for good measure, singer Matthew Healy reactivated an old Nik Kershaw haircut.'

The newspaper went on to say that for all those influences from bands, no one sounded quite like The 1975: 'No wonder the male half of the audience punched the air. At the centre of it all, as "Girls", "The City" and the earthquake that was "Chocolate" swirled around him, Healy was the oddest factor of all. What a strange, curiously charismatic little man he proved to be, whether moving like a mannequin, waltzing around his microphone or simply wandering across stage, lost in his own world, swigging from a bottle of wine. He was, of course, impossibly watchable.'

But things really came to a head two weeks later as the band returned to Manchester to play The Ritz, the cavernous ballroom venue just round the corner from Sound Control. 'I haven't really been back to Manchester this year – maybe once or twice, but we've been so busy,' Healy said in an interview with Dom Smith before the gig. 'We've been on tour this whole time and tonight at The Ritz is one of the shows that I've been looking forward to most this year. We played The Deaf Institute last time we came here, and now we're doing The Ritz! This is the first proper show of our own here, and it's going to be a real homecoming, I think.'

That night at The Ritz – chugging from a bottle of red wine onstage – Healy was in high spirits: 'Ladies and gentlemen, we are The 1975 and we're from fucking Manchester!' he told the audience. 'We've been away, but we return with a No.1 album… and that's thanks to you guys. So let's go!'

Music writer Alana Turk was there for the *Louder Than War* website to review the homecoming gig: 'The Ritz is absolutely packed – more filled out than I've ever seen it before – and the temperature is heating up before the gig has even started. The lights begin to dim and suddenly the room is filled with the sounds of "The 1975", the opening track of the band's self-titled debut. Huge cheers and whistles quickly drown out the music as the Mancunian four-piece enter the stage. Without a word, The 1975 open their set with debut single "The City". There is an immense energy emanating off the stage and into the audience. It is clear from the onset that this is going to be a fantastically atmospheric show.'

With shows in Manchester already booked for four months' time, Healy seemed acutely aware of how far the band had come in a very short space of time. 'Manchester, you have no idea how long we've worked for this show,' he told the crowd during their encore. 'Eight months ago we sold about 100 tickets for a show at Sound Control and we return to Manchester Academy in January, so thank you so much for that!'

SEVEN

AND THE WORST BAND IS...

In October 2013 the band uploaded a video for album track 'Girls' – director Adam Powell was back with the band, trying to send up The 1975's slightly pretentious image, eighties pop videos à la Robert Palmer's 'Addicted To Love', and the expectations of their fans all in one suspender-clad package. 'We set out to make a video about a band not wanting to make a video,' Powell told MTV. 'It's really funny to me, the impression people have of the music industry and music-video directors. It's fun to play with that image. This is really the first time I've had such a direct conversation with a fan base through my work. We're all kind of poking fun at each other, and it's a really great thing to be a part of. I had the best of both worlds, being able to make a full-on pop video but [to also] be kind of cheeky, silly and subversive, you know?'

Put another way, you get to send up the notion of having girls in their underwear in your videos... while also having girls in their underwear in your videos. Blur tried the same thing with their Benny Hill-themed video for 'Country House'.

'It was born of the video before it, which was born of the video before that,' Healy explained to *Spook* magazine. 'There was the original video for "Sex", which was black and white and got us a certain amount of popularity amongst our first hardcore cult following, when we were very esoteric and no one knew who we were. Then when we put "Sex" out as a single, and we thought, *Let's do another video for it, an album version of the video*, and when we made it, it looked better in colour, so we put it out and our fans then went fucking nuts.

'It started with anger, then it became bartering, and then it became that we were being compromised. It was, *Oh my god, they're completely conforming to a major label now*, which for us was so far from the truth that we thought, This is interesting. This is the first bit of conflict that we've had from our fans. So, we made a video about it. So, the "Girls" video was about a band who didn't want to make a colour video, who didn't want to be a pop band.'

The band returned to Manchester just before Christmas as part of XFM's Winter Wonderland show – a strange line-up that also included Jake Bugg and Primal Scream. The show was at the city's hefty Apollo venue, the kind of theatre The 1975 were very close to being able to play themselves. Inevitably, with a music scene as close-knit and insular as Manchester's

Top: The original line-up – Ross MacDonald, Adam Hann, Owen Davies, Matthew Healy and George Daniel.

(© Owen Davies, 2007)

Below: A young Matt Healy honing his art at a local gig.

Centre: Playing the Scu Bar for Pop Bubble Rock in February 2007.

(© Ben Hiard)

Right: Opening for Hundred Reasons and Jonny Foreigner, Manchester 2009.

(Flyer courtesy of Ben Hiard)

Bottom: Healy with his mum, Denise Welch arriving at the UK premiere of the Michael Jackson film, *The Life of an Icon* in 2011.

(Suzan Suzan/EMPICS Entertainment, 2011)

The 1975 play Sound Control in Manchester, 2012. After this gig, everything changed. *(© Emily Brinnand)*

Left: Dressed in white, head to toe – The 1975 perform on The Other Stage at Glastonbury 2016.

(© Richard Gray/EMPICS Entertainment)

Right: At The Mercury Music Prize, September 2016.

(© Matt Crossick/PA Wire)

Left: The 1975 play their emotional homecoming gig at Manchester Arena, December 2016.

(PA images, 2016)

there would be a certain amount of snootiness about the band's success – there is no musical city in Britain that does 'snooty' quite like Manchester. This was summed up by the write-up the band received on the *Manchester Confidential* website.

'I can't get on with The 1975,' wrote reviewer David Blake. 'Yes, they're local lads from Wilmslow but that shouldn't sway reasoned judgement. I find them irritating. I don't get it. It's like emo warmed up, or slightly tinkered (turns out that a couple of years back they were actually an emo band, until they realised everyone thought it was shit). Every lyric lead singer Matthew Healy (son of Tim) bleats out sounds, in a fashion, like he's fornicating. But struggling with the whole process.'

It didn't get any better: 'Onstage they're trying to convey that poetically dark and ghostly back-lit monochrome romanticism that The xx have done so very well and reinvent some kind of pop-punk nostalgia felt for late 90s/early 00s bands like New Found Glory or Jimmy Eat World, but never achieve the mediocre heights of either. It's awkward, tired and recycled. Radio 1 one-song hype. And I don't like the way their hair flaps about.'

It was inevitable that the band's growing status was going to rub some people up the wrong way in their adopted home city. The reality is that Manchester didn't actually pay The 1975 a great deal of attention until they broke through, by which time it was, in many ways, too late. 'There's proper Mancunian press people who don't like us because we don't sound like a Manchester band,' Healy told US journalist Andrew Unterberger. 'But what they're forgetting is the reason [those bands] were good was because they didn't sound like anything else. We don't sound like any other band from Manchester, ever. And that's what being a Manchester band is.'

It wouldn't be long before The 1975 were beyond the stage that reviewers in Manchester – or anywhere else for that matter – could deflect them from the task in hand. 'We live in our own vacuum, we're more worried about what the fans think than the press,' manager Jamie Oborne told industry journalist Rhian Jones. 'I get emails from kids telling me that the band's music saved their life. I'd rather get an email like that every day, which I do, than plaudits from people I don't know. Sometimes you work with artists and you almost don't have to do anything and you have momentum. It's always been like that with The 1975. It's amazing to have achieved what we have so far and be on the cusp of so much more.'

Meanwhile, the tour to support their album snaked around the UK and morphed into an ever-growing affair, with multiple nights being inserted into an already packed schedule. 'It's very, very humbling,' Healy told *Stereoboard*, using what was rapidly becoming his favourite word [humbling]. 'And it's very, very strange to think that there's that many people that want to come and see our shows. I think the only responsibility we have is to make them as entertaining and as emotional an experience as possible. I'm really excited about it because I think our band really works in a big room.'

By the end of 2013, Healy and the rest of the band – a group he'd once described as 'lazy stoners' – were in the position of knowing that virtually their every waking hour was accounted for over the following year. 'Who gets to have that much structure in their life? No one, really,' Healy told music journalist Kristina Osterling as 2014 approached. 'The fact that we're going to be playing a show pretty much every day next year is daunting, but it's pretty exciting. I'm just full of shit. I want what I don't have. When I get time off I don't want it. I can't sit still. I'm never happy.'

Healy's promise to return to Manchester at the city's Academy venue was upheld in January 2014 – but by now it had mushroomed into a three-night affair, proving that they could easily handle the city's big venues on their own. Just over a year on from attracting 150 people to their Sound Control gig half a mile away, The 1975 had sold nearly eight thousand tickets for their run of shows at the Academy in the heart of the city's studentland. With the now familiar bottle of red wine in hand, Healy told the sell-out local crowd: 'Boy, it's taken us a long time to get here…'

Reviewers were noticing how the band's show was now a much more considered, glossy affair. The days of Healy bringing along his own strobe light as he did when they were Drive Like I Do were long gone. 'It is just a short bus ride from the band's well-heeled hometown of Wilmslow to Manchester's Academy,' wrote The Independent, 'a place, Healy pointed out, where he and the lads had spent much time in attendance whilst trying their luck in teenage bands. Emerging amid the geometric lights and swirling dry ice on that stage on the first stop on a European and American tour, a No. 1 debut album already under their belt, must have felt like a triumph.'

But the upgrade in technology wasn't without its problems and on the third night, the show had to be stopped and restarted: 'We've been on tour for a year and haven't had a problem,' Healy told the crowd. 'Yet we come back to Manchester and mess it up. So we're going to try that again…'

'The tour's been amazing really,' he told music journalist Katie Skerritt. 'It's the first time we've done like a full show, you know? Like a proper 1975 show. Before this, the sets had been about forty minutes and we were a new band, so we weren't really expecting to headline shows. Now we've got all of the lights and everything. The live show is another facet of what we're about. One of the things with our band is that there's quite a lot of attention to detail in it. There's a synergy between the aesthetic and the music and stuff. I think the live show is very much in the vein of that, it's very stylised.'

The Manchester shows were followed by another three-nighter, this time at London's Brixton Academy. This time, fifteen thousand tickets were sold. At the end of the first night, after a riotous version of 'Sex' Healy jumped into the throng for a celebratory crowd surf – the crowd was so shocked it parted and the singer had to return to the stage. The reviews for their shows were by now coming from national newspapers, not just the music press and indie bloggers and most were coming round to The 1975's way of thinking.

'Healy and his tattooed, coiffed band mates oozed a kind of manicured rock 'n' roll chic: like a band straight from an Asos catalogue,' said the *Daily Telegraph*. 'That's not to say The 1975 were all hair mousse and no tunes. The quartet were a tightly sprung, well-oiled live unit, delivering overdriven, four-chord rock, pitched somewhere between Foals' arty indie, the dirgey post-punk of Echo and the Bunnymen and American emo bands like Fall Out Boy. When topped with catchy refrains about youthful excess and group harmony vocals, this made songs like "The City" and "She Way Out" irresistible.'

'You can't help but like The 1975,' said Hannah Britt in the *Daily Express*. 'They seem as excited to be playing the Brixton Academy as their fans are to watch them. The four-piece indie band from Wilmslow certainly had a good 2013. Releasing their self-titled debut album in September, they received both critical and fan acclaim. As someone who remembers them from growing up in Manchester, it was incredible to see how successful they had become. The band start their hour-and-a-half set at with "The City" and the crowd, an eclectic mix of screaming teenage girls and grown-up indie kids, loosen their checked shirts and go wild. From "Heart Out", complete with jazz saxophone, to their break-out hit "Chocolate", the set is lively and the boys have enough energy between them to power a small village.'

'If they are calculated, The 1975 are just the latest in a long line of tuneful magpies with no active sense of shame who have cunningly titled their singles after appealing things: "Girls", "Chocolate", "The City"," Sex",' said the *Guardian*. 'It really is no mystery why they are successful; but it's heartening to find that there is something more to The 1975 than funky surfaces.'

In the audience at one of the Brixton shows was none other than Drive Like I Do guitarist Owen Davies. He'd left Wilmslow and moved to London but had always stayed in touch with his former band mates. It was the first time he'd seen them live since their success had kicked in. 'I just remember standing there,' he told me. 'I just had a massive smile on my face for the whole thing, thinking… *This is incredible; everyone knows all the words to all the songs!* To look at them on that stage compared to the first gig at the Macclesfield Youth Bands, it's just two different worlds. I get friends kinda saying to me from time to time, "Oh you must be really gutted, or really annoyed", but genuinely, I'm not at all. It's not the path I was going to take anyway. I'm happy as can be and really proud of the guys.'

Meanwhile, fans concerned about the lack of black and whiteness in the band's last video for 'Girls' would have been more than pleased with the sheer volume of it involved with the promo for their next release, 'Settle Down'.

Like a supernatural *Kes* – the gritty, 1969 Ken Loach film showing the hopelessness of teenage life in a run-down community – it couldn't be further away from the thongs and pouts of 'Girls'. Directed by Danish-born Nadia Marquard

Otzen, the strange and bleak affair sees only Healy from the band appearing on screen. The rest of the time is spent following the lives of two separate but intertwined young boys in a monochrome Northern landscape. The idea was based on a recurring dream that Healy had as a child. 'I've dreamt the story of these two boys on countless occasions – every time drawing a different conclusion on its meaning,' he said in what was becoming one of his regular missives released alongside a new video. 'With "Settle Down" I wanted to make a story about the extension of that dream, a video that explores love, a video that was as fantastical, consuming and limitless as the love we all chase and desire. Love as I have always imagined. So upon meeting Nadia, who directed the video, I told her about my dream. We sat for hours looking through pictures and talking – it was decided in those moments. We were just to film my dream. The process of making this video was so intensely exciting for me as I was finally working through and figuring out exactly what this place, this story and these characters meant to me. I think now that I understand it. But I'm totally open to suggestions/interpretations.'

One thing that definitely wasn't open to interpretation was the award the band 'received' from the *NME* in March 2014 – that of Worst Band. The event took place at the Brixton Academy – the very venue that the band had sold out for three nights just a few weeks earlier. In amongst the usual gongs for Best British Band (Arctic Monkeys), Best Solo Artist (Lily Allen) and Godlike Genius (Blondie) were two rather pointless, negative awards: One Direction's Harry Styles was awarded Villain of the Year (for the second year running) and The 1975 were named Worst Band, taking over from last year's winners... One Direction. To add insult to injury, the ceremony was hosted by Radio 1's Huw Stephens, who was an early champion of The 1975.

What seemed to annoy Healy the most was the fact that he never actually received a physical award for being lead singer of the Worst Band. 'It's just quite funny – I never got that award, I was really annoyed,' he later told *Digital Spy*. 'I don't care, but I suppose if you make the forthright decision to give someone an award on a negative basis then you should do it! They didn't give it to us and they didn't even present it at the thing. Wolf Alice were gonna go up and pick it up for me. I don't really care and I think the *NME* don't really care that much. I grew up kind of being the antithesis of the *NME* anyway. Anything that they liked I didn't, so there's this weird kind of irony where I kind of embrace that award a little bit because all my subverting of the *NME* has now been validated in a concrete award. It's the cyclical nature of rock 'n' roll, as Alex Turner said at the Brits.'

Ironically, the band would play the *NME*/Radio 1 Stage at Reading later that year. What's more, the newspaper would later eat its words by fawning over The 1975 two years later when they released their second album. 'It's so over now,' Healy would later say. 'We're from different worlds and, you know, the *NME* don't slag us off; they had one pop at us with that award. They don't slag us off, they just don't seem to like us.'

Almost as if to stick two fingers up to the likes of the *NME*, Healy then revealed he was planning to work with none other than One Direction. The connection started after fellow Cheshire lad Harry Styles had tweeted his appreciation of an emotional, slow jam cover version of 'What Makes You Beautiful' that The 1975 had performed for Radio 1's Live Lounge. 'Loved the live lounge. And the album is ridiculous, So so good,' tweeted Styles to his 30 million followers.

Much to the delight of the gossip pages, it seemed they had a full-on bromance on their hands. 'He's cool – he's become a little bit of a mate of mine, that Harry Styles,' Healy told Freedom Radio. 'I don't know how, but he kind of got my number to say how much he liked our album. I ended up texting him, "Thanks for tweeting about it, that was really sweet."'

Bromances were one thing, but a collaboration? That could really set the cash registers ringing. None other than Healy's mum confirmed that the collaboration was on: 'He's writing a song for them,' Denise Welch told *Digital Spy*. 'I'm friends with Harry Styles's mum, Anne. I always know when she's tweeted me because I've got 27,000 of the 1D army and the 1975 army [on my timeline] and they go into meltdown.'

Some felt that such a pairing might drag The 1975 too close to the mainstream, and Healy himself seemed slightly wary of the idea when asked about it. 'I went down and met them and started to work on a track,' the singer told *News.com* in

Australia, where the band had headed after their latest UK dates. 'I don't know what's going on because we are the busiest band in the world along with One Direction. So to get me and one of One Direction in the same room is going to be a fucking nightmare. But I'm going to write them a song – it's not going to be One Direction featuring me. I spend a lot of my time in The 1975 trying to rein in my love of pop. I have to make sure everything is pitched slightly left of centre, so to be smack bang in the middle and writing straight pop [for One Direction] is going to be interesting. But if it is massive – I'll probably be defined by that one track, which will be really weird.'

The song in question – 'Change Your Ticket' – was a very 1975-flavoured affair indeed and appeared as a bonus track on the 'Ultimate Edition' of One Direction's *Four* album. But it wasn't a Healy co-write at all. He wasn't involved and seemed slightly annoyed he'd been brought in under somewhat false pretences: 'They got me in, and they said, "We really like your band. Would you write a song for us?"' he explained to Andrew Unterberger. 'They didn't seem to be actually that interested [in writing a song]; they just wanted to play me this song that they said was really, really inspired by us.'

The song's similarity to The 1975's sound – particularly the breezy guitar funk of 'Girls' – did not go down well with Healy, who asked them to tone down the 1975-isms a touch. Healy told them: 'Listen, guys, fill your boots, the song doesn't sound *that* much like "Girls". But the guitar and the whole vibe of it is a complete lift. So take the guitars off, and we're good.'

When the song appeared, the 1975 vibe and the 'Girls'-style guitars were still very much in evidence. Healy also seemed particularly miffed that the impression was given that he'd had a hand in writing the song, which is actually a co-write between 1D and, amongst others, David Guetta and Maroon 5 collaborator Sam Martin. 'It would have been a bad 1975 song,' was Healy's view. The issue was explained away as a management 'mix-up' and the singer said he bore no grudge against One Direction... but Healy being Healy, he couldn't resist a final dig: 'Oh, well... they're four guys who queued up outside an arena to sing in front of Simon Cowell. Do they really have any artistic credibility? That sounds like a mean thing to say, but it's a good question. Like, *do they?*'

The situation didn't appear to affect Healy's friendship with Styles. In May he played a prank on the One Directioner for the benefit of Radio 1; Healy claimed he needed some cash double-quick to get him out of sticky situation: 'Basically I need five grand,' he told Styles, as the conversation was secretly recorded for Nick Grimshaw's breakfast show. 'I'm in Chalk Farm [North London] and I'm having an emergency... it's actually quite a serious situation. I've got two guys in here in a phone box with me, one of them just keeps pointing at a photo of Mark Owen [of Take That]. It's really weird, I don't know what that means, and it's really threatening. Do you reckon you could get Niall to come down and sort me the cash?' To Styles' credit, he agreed to stump up the cash with very little fuss, proving that all was well between the two, if nothing else.

After touring Australia in the New Year, The 1975's reputation as a fearsome road machine was further enhanced by putting on gigs in Japan before another UK tour and a tour of Ireland. Then there were shows in France, Italy, Germany, Switzerland, Luxembourg and the US. An astonishing work rate. Surely The 1975 were by now one of the hardest-working bands on the world touring circuit?

At the end of March they even did a short tour of shopping malls in the Philippines, holding a press conference beforehand to introduce themselves to the local press and fielding questions about what kind of girls they liked. 'The thing we took away was just how much more intense it was than anywhere else in the world, fan-wise,' guitarist Adam Hann later told *Inquirer.net*. 'It was the most fanatical response we've ever had, and probably still to this day, really.'

As they criss-crossed the planet Healy was fast becoming a figure of intense and in some cases, extreme attention for the band's followers – they would shower him with gifts, many of them with deep-seated significance to the individual fan. These gifts would literally become a burden for the singer: 'Fans really put a lot into the idea of who you are,' Healy revealed to *GQ*. 'Kids have, like, given me *razor blades*. When you're presented with that, it's so intense. I know that shit must happen to other pop stars but I always say I literally tour with emotional baggage. I collect everything that these kids give me, and I have to buy a suitcase every time I leave a country for other people's emotional stuff that I take home and try to read through. But I think I put myself out there and I'm really honest, so to tell somebody not to be honest with me would almost be hypocritical.'

Healy's suitcase must have been bulging as he and the band returned to Britain to play one of the world's most iconic venues – London's Royal Albert Hall. 'We couldn't get fifty people to come to see one of our shows in Manchester in 2011, now we're headlining the Royal Albert Hall,' he marvelled to the *musicOMH* video channel. 'It's the most beautiful, prestigious music venue ever. All the greats have played there. The week we're playing it's Suede, The Cure are playing three nights, then it's us.'

Built in 1871, the iconic venue has played host to everything from the BBC Proms to the English National Ballet, the Teenage Cancer Trust to The Royal British Legion Festival of Remembrance. The 5,000-plus capacity hall is one of the most respected venues in the world. So when Matthew Healy and friends stepped out to meet the crowd in April 2014, they treated it with the kind of reverence it deserved: 'To all the people who said this band would never do anything,' Healy said, 'welcome to the fucking Royal Albert Hall!'

'One wouldn't expect the four grubby boys from Manchester who made their London debut at The Barfly less than eighteen months ago to be selling out the Royal Albert Hall on a Sunday night,' said the review of the show on the *When The Gramophone Rings* music website. '[But] it becomes abundantly clear this show is every bit a celebration for both the band and the fans that have taken them there, as each member of the quartet beams with a poignant mix of emotion and excitement throughout the set, with every track receiving an increasingly passionate response from the audience.

'If there was any indicator that The 1975 had well and truly "made it", this show was it, and there was no better setting. Few bands can hold an audience in the palm of their hand quite like this four-piece, and whilst every element of their live show seems gargantuan and fitting for the festival headline slots that will no doubt await them in the coming years, there is still a refreshing sense of naivety and emotion on display, which ultimately leaves us rooting for them throughout, and will continue to for years to come.'

In May, 'Robbers' was released as a stand-alone track from the album, the sixth song to be taken from their debut. Once again, Healy is the focus of the promo, making a reasonable fist of playing a coked-out armed robber, one half of a Bonnie and Clyde-style couple. Once again, the inspiration came from a film, in this case the Quentin Tarantino-scripted 1993 movie *True Romance* starring Christian Slater as an Elvis-obsessed criminal and Patricia Arquette as his call-girl moll. 'I got really obsessed with the idea behind the characters in *True Romance* when I was about eighteen,' Healy told MTV. 'That craving for the bad boy in that film, it's so sexualised. It was something I was obsessed with. "Robbers" is about a heist that goes wrong – I suppose you can read it as a metaphor – and a girl who's obsessed with her professional killer boyfriend. It's a romantic ideal.'

The video for 'Robbers' was directed by Tim Mattia, who'd also shot the re-vamped version of 'Sex'. Although not a huge seller as a single – perhaps because half a dozen songs had by now been lifted from the album – 'Robbers' racked up tens of millions of online hits for its video, which contains references that would pop up in future The 1975 promos. Healy was now so involved with the video-making process, it was sometimes difficult to tell where he and the director divided up the responsibilities: 'I write all the videos and have mates who are brilliant directors,' he explained to the BBC. 'I write the storyline when I'm writing the song and how I see it in my head. It gives continuity.'

Healy does a pretty decent job of waving a gun around and being a terrible robber in the video, prompting inevitable questions about whether he fancied his chances as a performer outside of music. 'People ask, "Do you want to follow your parents into acting?" Like you just follow them without any hard work! I really struggled with that. Being an actor is such hard work.'

The 'Robbers' video ends with Healy covered in blood, suffering from a gunshot wound after his character's robbery goes wrong. It's not clear whether he lives or dies. A similar problem would hit Healy himself that summer, when a rumour swept the Internet that he'd actually died in real life. What's worse, as the subject of his apparent demise was trending, he was offline and out of contact, meaning he wasn't able to stop the rumour in its tracks. 'Someone said I had an overdose in my flat,' he told *Bang Showbiz*. 'Who's making that shit up? I didn't. I was on a plane to America. My mum rang me in tears. She thought I was dead for six hours. That's not cool at all. That is the shit I don't like [about fame].'

Meanwhile, as the festival season got underway, the band had a full calendar of outdoor shows in Britain and continental Europe. But it would be a return to the Glastonbury Festival in June that would provide the backdrop to another example of the downside of being a famous band. The 1975 had been slotted in to play a secret set on the William's Green Stage prior to their main appearance. Metronomy had agreed to appear, too. But the mood turned ugly during The 1975's set, with Healy warning someone who was throwing missiles at the stage and heckling. Fights were breaking out too. It would be another instance of Healy's no-nonsense stagecraft – hard earned in the pubs and bars of Manchester – coming into play: 'Throw one more fucking thing, mate, and I don't care if it's Glastonbury, I'll come down there and kick your fucking head in!'

When the singer was hit by a can from the same section of the audience, enough was enough. Healy threw down his guitar and jumped into the crowd to sort things out, with other band members following. Soon after, a man was ejected by security. Healy apologised to the 'peace-loving members of Glastonbury', before pointing at the exiting missile-thrower and saying, 'Throw shit at me and I'll fuck you up! Fuck him and his mates! It's not in the spirit, is it?'

The band's Sunday-afternoon appearance on The Pyramid Stage was an altogether more good-natured affair: 'Let's have a fuckin' dance, Glastonbury!' exhorted Healy as the band played their mid-afternoon slot before country-and-western star Dolly Parton played the traditional late-afternoon 'legends' slot. The band possibly achieved an even bigger crowd, thanks to those who were there for Parton. Healy helpfully provided updates for those waiting for her: 'She's backstage,' he told the crowd, 'trying to get off with Ed Sheeran.'

Parton played to the biggest crowd of the festival that day – she was the undisputed hit of Glastonbury – but she still took a moment beforehand to show her appreciation of Matthew Healy. 'All the other bands playing lined up by the side of the stage and clapped as Dolly went on, like she was the Queen,' Healy later told the *New York Post*. 'She gave me a wink as she went! Unfortunately, being from the generation I am, I wasn't as impressed by that as I would be if it had been Beyoncé – which is sad. But it was still a big deal.'

Healy, of course, had set himself the challenge of headlining The Pyramid Stage by 2016 – if nothing else, they could do with playing later in the day so their light show could kick in. A muddy field – quite possibly with the rain coming on – was not necessarily the natural habitat for The 1975. 'Festivals can be a nightmare for us,' Healy confessed to *Billboard*. 'Our band is based on theatrics and grandeur and glamour. There's a lot of moving parts in our show. Obviously we have a responsibility to be as professional as possible, and in those situations people come there to enjoy themselves and have music be a release for them. If you start stressing out onstage it kills everyone's vibe. So if everything's going down you just have to embrace it and let it go wrong and feel like people aren't going to judge you as long as you slog through it and do your best to give them what they came for.'

'They don't look out of place here,' was the *Guardian*'s slightly begrudging verdict of The 1975's Glastonbury set. 'Healy, in particular, revels in the attention given to him by a larger audience. The tunes help: "Chocolate" and "Sex" already feel like laser-guided festival sing-alongs. Yet the criticism often levelled at The 1975 – that they're synth pop by committee, and a little too slick – ignores the fact that, at heart, they're actually a bit weird: *Seinfeld* slap bass rubs up against echoey R&B tones and boy-band harmonies while a saxophone parps wildly away in the background. It's only token ballad "Robbers" that feels calculated and familiar here, and it might be the biggest hit of all with this Pyramid crowd, who sway approvingly along in the mid-afternoon haze.'

The band continued their epic trek through the music festivals across Britain and beyond, racking up appearances in Norway, Finland, Portugal, Latvia, Romania, Japan and even Seoul. They also, inevitably, returned to Manchester. The venue would be another indication of their growing popularity: the Manchester Apollo. The last time they were there it was to share a bill with Jake Bugg and Primal Scream; this time they'd been booked to play it under their own steam. A great art-deco barn of a venue that sits on the edge of Manchester in Ardwick, the Apollo had long been the preserve of the higher level of touring bands. With its 3,500 capacity you need to be big to play the Apollo.

For Healy – a serious student of live music – the symbolic aspect of playing the venue was all too obvious: 'When we did the Apollo in Manchester, I sat at the dressing room window from 10 o'clock in the morning and I watched as every single kid turned up, because I know what it's like to go to a show there,' he later explained to *Dork* magazine. 'I know what buses you have to get it you want to go from Wythenshawe or Cheadle. I know what it's like when you come out the Apollo and your ears are ringing and you get in your dad's car and it's deathly silent and the indicators sound insanely loud and you're really sweaty. The amount of history I had with the Apollo, I sat there and I really appreciated it. I really got it and I really felt…*fucking hell, this is full circle.*

As the September dates approached, The 1975 had been booked to play not one but *two* nights at the venue. Not only could they handle the likes of the Apollo, they were being talked about as a potential arena act. 'Watching the group at a packed Apollo one thing became instantly clear; their popularity amongst teenage girls is unparalleled,' wrote the reviewer for the *Manchester Evening News.* 'For anyone who has ever watched grainy footage of The Beatles performing in their heyday, with hundreds of teens screaming and fainting, a gig with The 1975 is a pretty similar experience. If the band continues with the momentum they have gathered so far it wouldn't be a surprise if they're selling out stadiums before long.'

As usual with Manchester shows, it was a sprawling, emotional affair with Healy even reading out an email from a group of fans who had asked if the band would dedicate a song to one of their mates. He had been due to be at one of the gigs, but had tragically taken his own life at the age of just twenty. 'I don't want to bring anybody down, but that shit really affected me,' the singer told the crowd, before breaking into 'Chocolate'. 'So this song's for Sam… it isn't about death – it's about smoking weed and fucking.'

Meanwhile, the final track from the band's debut album was released – fan favourite 1980s stomper 'Heart Out'. With perhaps a nod to their youth-club beginnings, the band were 'seen' performing in a talent show after a dance troop. As was by now becoming a tradition, Healy put out his thoughts behind the idea behind the video: 'With the video for "Heart Out" I wanted to return to the classic performance scene. I love a good performance video and wanted to try my hand at creating something that represented my grandeur and slightly deluded sense of self, whilst also adhering to the simplistic rules of a performance. The video is about narcissism, belief and delusion in equal measure. It represents how antiquated and romanticised visions of past and future shed a blazing light on the present and in turn provoke a self-analysis that soon shifts from the material to the ideological. It was in this state of excitement and obsession where the "Heart Out" video was born. Obviously I can delve into the artistic vision of the video – what it means to me, the subtext and my own emotional investment within it – but in doing so I fear defacing what the video truly is about, at face value. It's a bunch of kids who think they're rock stars. And… they are.'

This turned out to be a slightly high-falutin' way of saying: *'The band didn't actually appear in the video; the well-worn technique of using kid lookalikes was used instead.'*

Queen had used the same idea in their video for 'It's A Miracle'; in 'Heart Out' the stand-in 1975 are correct down to mini-Matthew's tattoos and mohawk as they wow a bunch of parents in a local hall.

The fact that the song was clearly signalled as the last to be culled from their debut album generated an obvious question: when is the new stuff coming? 'There have been times when I've not had the environment to write in the way I used to,' Healy told *Gigwise* when asked about the likelihood of new material. 'I never used to write just on an acoustic guitar, but I found myself doing that. There's a couple of songs that are really, really personal and acoustic, but there's a lot of R&B eighties-inspired pop music on there. It sounds a bit like Bobby Brown at the moment, Alexander O'Neal. That sort of thing.'

Questions about what the new tracks might sound like would be partially answered with the release of 'Medicine' in late October. It was part of an unusual project curated by then

Radio 1 tastemaker Zane Lowe to create a new soundtrack for the 2011 cult Ryan Gosling film *Drive*. Lowe would unveil the tracks on his show before the rescored film was shown that month on BBC Three.

Chvrches, Foals and Bring Me the Horizon were also on board for the project. The track contributed by The 1975 was in fact credited to just Healy and Daniel. For someone like Healy, who'd spent so long comparing his band's music to an imaginary soundtrack, it must have been a beguiling proposition to actually appear on such a project: 'We wrote "Medicine" for our chosen scenes,' he said at the time of the film's showing. '"Medicine", its title and sentiment, goes all the way back to the original The 1975 project that was based in my bedroom. It's a new piece of music informed by the genesis of our band and our love for *Drive* as a film… The movie itself plays with the duality of resignment and hope – and this is most obvious and stirring in the scenes we chose to score. The song is a testament to that same idea and has in turn become one of our most personal and best loved pieces of music to date.'

The film's director, Nicolas Winding Refn, gave the project his blessing, describing the process in a way that would surely have appealed to Matthew Healy. 'It's like going through your drawers and finding the greatest pot,' he told journalists in a live Q&A prior to the film's transmission. 'You inhale it and it's so great again, except different five years later. I consider it a great honour that my movie *Drive* inspired so many wonderful artists to come together and create one ultra-cool glam experience.'

Zane Lowe was typically bullish about the project: 'Honestly, this is the most exciting thing that this show has ever been involved in,' he enthused just prior to transmission. 'It's the most ambitious, awesome thing we've ever done. We've been working on it all year and we're super-proud of it – you don't want to miss this!'

Sadly, not everyone was quite so pumped up about the idea. Kat Brown in the *Daily Telegraph* – who named 'Medicine' as the best of the contributions – said, 'It was a valiant effort, but I'm none the wiser as to why. Lowe's curation left no particular stamp on it beyond sounding quite similar. It was like someone choosing to dress up as the *Drive* soundtrack for Halloween, only there wasn't anything funny or smart about it, and no sweets or alcohol changed hands. There's clearly a market for putting a new stamp on films, but it has to be a real mark. That really didn't happen tonight.'

Filmic experiments aside, what people really wanted to know was, were the band working on a new album? And what would it be like? 'The first album was about coming to terms with your adolescence,' Healy explained to *Radio.com*. 'This [new] record is about the excitement and the apprehension and the cacophony of this world and this industry and all of the things that come with being a new band. A rising new band. That's what people want to hear, right?'

EIGHT

249724 KILOMETRES

If you're British, have tattoos, can sing, or possess a guitar – or at the very least have access to one – then it's very likely that at some stage you'll be romantically linked to US pop siren Taylor Swift. It's almost like a test of whether your pop culture stock is on the rise. In the late autumn of 2014, this is exactly what happened to Matthew Healy.

Swift and Healy first met in October of that year as Healy left Britain and began criss-crossing Europe on The 1975's latest tour. Always an open book, Healy admitted he was interested in the singer, who'd already been linked to Harry Styles and Ed Sheeran, amongst others. 'I met Taylor Swift, that was really nice,' he said. 'We exchanged numbers. Let's see what happens. I mean, what am I going to do? Go out with Taylor Swift? She's a sensation. I wouldn't say no.'

Swift went to see The 1975 twice in November. At the first gig in Los Angeles she was accompanied by actress Selena Gomez; Swift posted a video online showing herself and Gomez singing along to 'The City' accompanied by the words, 'If you wanna find love. Then you know where the city is #the1975.'

If nothing else, Healy was able to witness the sheer star power of someone like Swift up close – it was a slightly unsettling experience: 'She came to our show, and you would have thought that Barack Obama had come out,' Healy later told *Rolling Stone*. 'I don't know another person on the planet that would elicit that kind of reaction. Maybe Kanye, but not even him… It's weird.'

Swift saw the band again in New York. On the second occasion – just to ramp things up a little – she turned up with Victoria's Secret models Lily Aldridge and Martha Hunt. Things went into another gear when Swift was seen wearing a The 1975 T-shirt just days after Healy was seen in one of Swift's *1989* tops.

The US media were starting to get very interested indeed in Matthew Healy. But things really kicked off after an Instagram video appeared showing the two together. In it, Healy promises a surprise for the daughter of his manager, Jamie Oborne… then pulls Swift into view. Result: meltdown.

Suddenly an awful lot of people who didn't know who Matthew Healy and The 1975 were very quickly did. And they weren't writing about the band and their music: 'This is just the CUTEST! Not to mention further proof of these two being an item,' gushed online gossip merchant Perez Hilton, not some-one who was normally in the habit of writing about The 1975. 'Taylor Swift has continually denied that she and Matthew Healy, the lead singer of The 1975, are dating, but this Instagram video seems to prove otherwise. In it, Matthew is saying hello to Kitty, the daughter of Jamie Oborne – aka the owner of The 1975's record label – when he pulls T. Swift in to say hi to her as well! In other words, a totally adorable moment that was all caught on video! We love it! They're just too cute together! They totally look like they could possibly, probably, definitely be dating! What do YOU think???'

When the pair were later photographed together in London – although, to be fair, Radio 1 DJ Nick Grimshaw was in between them – at a Universal Music party, it seemed a done deal. Healy appeared dazed by the whole process, although not so much that he couldn't recognise the potential benefits. 'I don't do anything else,' he told Q magazine in 2016. 'So it doesn't leave a lot of room for me going out, or shagging someone. So the one time I did have a flirtation with a girl it ends up going everywhere. I mean, I got on *E! News* and people were like, Who's Matthew Healy? So that was cool. But I didn't make a big deal out of it myself. It's not really anything to talk about, because if she wasn't Taylor Swift we wouldn't be talking about her. She wasn't a big impact on my life.

'It's just interesting to me. If I had [properly] gone out with Taylor Swift, I would've been, *Fucking hell, I am not being Taylor Swift's boyfriend!* You know, Fuck. That. That's also a man thing, a de-masculinating, emasculating thing.'

The 'emasculating' comment would come back to bite Healy, with columnists and commentators having a field day tearing the statement – and Healy himself – to bits. 'Just to make ourselves clear, saying that it's a weakness to get involved with a woman who is considered powerful or commanding is SUPER OFFENSIVE,' wrote MTV's Charlotte Warwick. 'Women absolutely shouldn't dim their amazing lights just so an insecure man can feel like they're shining brighter than her. Yes, most of us like to have our #GIRLBOSS pants on a lot of the time, so if that's an issue, we'll happily lose out on the likes of Matthew.'

It would be inevitable that interest would swirl around someone like Healy and his personal life – though the press had been surprisingly coy when it came to his previous relationship with fashion model Gemma Janes, who he'd met on a video shoot, despite the fact she would sometimes sit in on interviews and post photos of the two of them on social media.

Meanwhile, as well as annoying MTV, Healy seemed to be doing a grand job of annoying the more conservative aspects of America. One show in Minnesota prompted one writer to openly declare that parents shouldn't let their youngsters anywhere near Healy and friends. Under the headline: WHY YOUR KIDS SHOUDN'T LISTEN TO THE 1975, the review laid out the full horror of the band's corrupting influence on the nation's youth.

'Healy walks out and the crowd loses it,' wrote Bo Weber after the band's gig in Maplewood. 'He makes his way to the edge of the stage holding a bottle of booze in his right hand. With people screaming for him, Matthew raises the bottle above his head – the cheering became louder. At this point, I'm wishing I had purchased earplugs. Three quarters into the show, the band ends one of their songs and the lights go out. Enough time goes by to where it seems as if the band is provoking an encore chant. Right on time, their teenage fans began chanting "WE WANT SEX!" …'

At one point during the gig Healy asked the crowd to put their cell phones away. The reviewer was impressed: 'I enjoyed that he was making an attempt to assess the technology overload of people's everyday lives. But! Just as he finished asking them to put their phones away, he lights up a cigarette, and the crowd goes wild, once again. There goes a good chunk of money that helpful organisations have spent on anti-smoking advertisements.

'I know what you're thinking, "He's a rock star, what do you expect?" Superstars like Rolling Stones, The Beatles and The Doors have promoted drugs and alcohol for years. Some might even say the rock-star lifestyle is as natural as the music itself. Let's change the perspective. You are a musician. Not just a musician; a pop star. Thousands watching you each night. You see the age of your fan base. You understand your sole ability of affecting a mass amount of young people in whatever way you wish. My question is, why promote addiction? If it's up to anyone to make a serious change in this world, it's in the hands of the people our children look up to: The artists.'

Whatever the rights and wrongs of Matthew Healy's ability to bring about a decline in morals in and around Minnesota, there was clearly a lot going on in his head towards the end of 2014. Their schedule was crushing by anyone's standards and he was finding himself the subject of the kind of attention – either about his love life or his position of corrupter of a nation's youngsters – that can't have been easy to handle.

Matters seemed to come to a head in Boston at the band's House of Blues show on 6 December. A teary and emotional Healy talked to the crowd about how they'd been on tour for two years. As was becoming the norm, audience members shouted their love for the singer throughout the show. For some reason, one girl's shout of 'I love you' seemed to upset Healy. An on-the-spot report from student newspaper *The Pentucket Profile* by Kelly Murray described what happened next: 'When a fan in the crowd shouted to the singer that she loves him, Matty simply responded, "Trust me you don't. You love the idea." The band continued the set and fans attempted to look past Matty's previous remarks, in hopes that he was having an off night, but it was later proven to be more than that as the singer began collapsing onstage, crying and even talking to himself.'

But it was during Healy's take on 'Is There Somebody Who Can Watch You' – the song written for his younger brother Louis about their parents' break-up – that things went from bad to worse: 'A single spotlight was beaming on Matty as he sat at his piano, preparing to perform,' the review continued. 'The concern of the fans began before the song had started when Matty whispered into his mic, "I just want to go home." He had only made it to the end of the first verse before his first real emotional breakdown. Seeing it firsthand, Matty buried his face in his hand and had to take a breather from his performance before returning to his personal state, ignoring all cheers and yells from the crowd. After the song, Matty was never the same and it was clear that the night had been a night of emotional breakdown for him. Fans on Twitter commented that he had "hit rock bottom in Boston last night" and "watching Matty have to be picked up and guided out after the show" was a lot to take in.'

In retrospect, the singer was appalled by what had happened. 'There was girl stuff. There was family stuff. There was financial stuff. There was drug stuff,' Healy later said, trying to explain the meltdown in an interview with the *Guardian*. 'I remember hearing the crowd and having an identity crisis. I thought: If you want to see a show, I'll give you a fucking show. If you've come to see the jester drink himself into a slumber, I'll give it to you. I felt like I'd become an idea as opposed to being a person. What did I say to the poor fucking girl? *You don't have the right to love me. You don't know me. I love you but you don't get to love me?* Jesus. Can you imagine your favourite band shouting that at you? What a dickhead. What a horrible thing to say to a kid who fucking does love me. George carried me off, 'cos I would have stayed there, apparently. I just wanted to sit there… It was so blurry and of such a particular colour: I remember everything as orangey yellow.'

The fact that it was Healy's 'other half' George Daniel who led the singer offstage said a great deal about their relationship. But it marked a turning point. 'I felt slightly out of control, as we'd always been the biggest influence in each other's lives,' Daniel later told music journalist Laura Barton. 'But we were under a lot of pressure and I don't think we believed in ourselves at that point. It was an odd time.'

'I love George like a husband,' said a chastened Healy. 'And those are the only things that keep bands together – when there's this mutual understanding of having each other's back. But that changed for the first time ever. Because I was off getting high. And George… he got so upset that I would lie to him. Because I'd never lied to him before. And there was this real, visceral reality that came over me that where I just kind of got my priorities right. I felt truly humbled.'

Although Healy was back onstage two days later as the tour continued – and his bottle of wine was back in its usual place in the singer's hand – the event marked a change in the band's attitude and schedule. If proof were needed about how hard The 1975 had worked recently, it came in the form of research by music website *Songkick*: The 1975 were officially the hardest-working band in the world. They'd played more shows than any other band in 2014. What's more, they'd done more gigs in the space of a year than any other act had managed since 2010. The statistics were as revealing as they were eye-watering: they played 195 shows in 29 countries, travelling 249,724 kilometres and lapping the world six times over. Their nearest rivals were fellow electro poppers Future Islands, then New Politics, Against Me! and St. Vincent.

With that kind of schedule, no wonder Healy just wanted to 'go home' by December 2014. The band released a statement to acknowledge the achievement: 'Touring this past year has been a really humbling experience. Our album was pretty much the story of the last decade of our lives, to see so many people around the world connecting with it has been incredible. We are very proud of our fans, they really understand what we are doing and the shows are an extension of that feeling.'

But the video of Healy's onstage meltdown had been seen far and wide. His onstage persona of the rock 'n' roll rake – shirt open, fag on the go, with a bottle of red wine super-glued to his hand – lead to concern about his well-being. He was heading out of his mid-twenties, a dangerous age for any rock star. 'I mean, day to day, I'm fine,' Healy later reasoned in an interview with *Spook* magazine. 'I'm not like, a walking nervous breakdown. Ideologically, I don't know, I guess I'm pretty fucked up. Like, I don't really know what to think. I can deal with it, I'm content, but I don't know what to make of it. Because where all of my music comes from is a place that – obviously there's ego and there's being a bit of a show-off – but it comes from quite a humble, self-aware, self-deprecating place; which is why all these teenagers love the ideas that are in the music. But I'm still quite neurotic, as everybody is. So, when you're really, really objectified and you don't have time off or time away from that and you're on tour for two and a half years, and every time you get up there's constant reminders of your projected personality.'

The shows would continue into the New Year, but The 1975's 2015 touring schedule was considerably lighter than 2014. The price of becoming The Hardest-working Band in the World had been a high one: 'Beginning in January [2015] we realised how much it really affected us,' George Daniel would later tell *Rolling Stone*. Daniel also lost confidence in his abilities as a producer on the upcoming album. 'We were just expecting this resolve when we finished touring. It was so easy to be stressed and miserable. We were all left with this existential nonsense surrounding everything we were doing. You realise it's three years later in your life and you don't know what happened. It's quite a naive thing to say, we were all mental for a while. I just didn't really feel qualified to make a record. I didn't feel ready and I didn't feel the conviction to get the job done.'

It was down to Healy, as usual, to talk up preparations for the second album: if nothing else, there was the small matter of a second album to deal with. 'We've been [writing] quite a lot and there's a lot of new music for the next record – but I'm not supposed to talk about it at the moment,' he told *Billboard* at the end of 2014, as usual not doing as he was told. 'We don't even know what it is yet, really. It needs time to become its own thing. We've got a very good idea of what's going on, but that could change, too.' The goal, he said, was to, 'put out an album two years to the day when we put out the last one – or at least as close as we can get. So it will come out on a Monday in September of 2015.'

It was a typically bold claim from Healy – as it turned out, it was an incorrect one.

* * *

In the spring of 2015, Healy kept – by his standards as least – a relatively low profile. He still managed to get himself all over the tabloids when he was photographed 'getting cosy' with TV presenter Caroline Flack at a record industry party in London. He even managed to get his picture taken with his hand over his face – in classic paparazzi style – as he left the party with Flack, who had previously been linked to Harry Styles. Showbiz writers couldn't believe their luck: 'Caroline Flack gets cosy with a lavish-haired rocker in his twenties – wait, doesn't that ring a bell?' wrote the *Mirror*. 'The *Strictly Come Dancing* champ, thirty-five, seemed to fall for the charms of twenty-five-year-old Matthew Healy, the son of former *Loose Women* star Denise Welch, at a Brits after-party this week. Caroline previously dated Harry Styles, fourteen years her junior, and last year split from music producer Jack Street, who is eight years younger than her. But she had eyes only for Matthew – frontman of rock band The 1975 – as they enjoyed champagne with friends at the Warner Music party.'

As the band took things a little easier, Healy was also able to head north and see his family – he and brother Louis went to watch their mum in a play in Bolton. He got snapped by the press as he went to see *The Ancient Secret of Youth and the Five Tibetans* at Bolton's Octagon Theatre, but seemed to take it in good spirit: 'It's great, I always love seeing my mum,' he told reporters. 'The play has got quite a tone to it.' Tellingly, in the piece accompanying the photos, Welch was referred to as being Healy's mum, rather than him being referenced as the 'son of *Loose Women* star' Denise Welch; by early 2015, Matthew Healy was becoming more famous than his famous mum.

Meanwhile, with some hefty gaps in their usually unrelenting tour schedule, the band were able to concentrate on their second album: 'We had the luxury of being able to spend four months in the studio in LA recording it,' Adam Hann told *Premier Guitar*. 'I feel like that's an amount of time not many people get in the studio nowadays. We're really quite lucky to have been able to go away for that long and really focus on each individual aspect and get it right.'

The confidence – particularly from drummer and co-producer George Daniel – was back. It was contagious and had spread to producer Mike Crossey too. Calling it 'the best thing I've ever done', Crossey said the band were embracing their magpie tendencies to flit and change between genres and styles at will. 'I think this amalgam of styles and sounds is part of the band's overall fingerprint,' he told US journalist Daniel Topete. 'When we get the feel right, it starts to become a 1975 song.'

As the summer approached, some people may have

remembered Healy's promise to produce the second album two years to the day after their debut had appeared. But instead of just a cartoon flyer or a flight of fancy missive from Healy, the band then pulled one of their oldest tricks. In the old days, early fans would notice how videos and songs would be deleted from the Internet, as if to create a sense of mystery. On Sunday, 31 May they did it again, but on a much grander scale.

In the afternoon of the 31st, Healy posted a cryptic cartoon flyer, which referenced Oasis, Nirvana and had a go at the band's thorn-in-the-side, the *NME* – 'Nihilistic Music Expression' as the paper was described. There was a fairly strong suggestion in the bizarre message that this was the end for The 1975. A black-clad figure is seen holding a pink figure; the first is marked 'old Matty', the second 'new Matty'. The flyer's text reads:

> 'Our projected identity must change not only visually but philosophically – how do you do that? Firstly we must reclaim our identity & repossess our control of it. It's simple. You could say it's black & white. Until then there won't be any pop music or dancing with long hair. 'You can't do that,' I hear you say. 'That's ours!' Correct!! The hardest part of any relationship is to say goodbye. As much as we would like things to stay the same, change is an inevitable part of life. We can't simply go on forever,

always staying the same. Never evolving. So we must leave, with a parting 'we love you' – we are already gone.'

At midnight that Sunday, all four members deleted their social-media accounts along with the band's online presence: The 1975 had gone. 'So, me and Jamie [Oborne] were talking about how we fuck around with the Internet, because the Internet's boring,' Healy later explained to MTV. 'And do we want to be a band that puts up a picture of their album, and then everyone goes, Hey, did you see The 1975 put out a new record? Oh, cool, yeah, cool – and then it's over within 10 hours. Or do we go back to our idea of desire being far more potent than obtaining something? Afterwards I was a bit like, *Oh, fuck, I've played with these kids a little bit.* But remember, I'd also been out of The 1975 for six months making the record in the studio. I hadn't been on Tumblr and Twitter and I wasn't thinking about it. So I just thought, Well, yeah, delete it, it'll be wicked! Just fuckin' delete it.'

There was online silence until the following night, when all the accounts were reactivated. The main band account reappeared with a pink version of a logo featuring their name in a rectangle, then with news that a new album was on the way, along with a tour. Healy took the opportunity of the temporary silence to put out a lengthy statement:

I/We/The 1975 are currently in production of our second full-length record. Its creation signifies the end of the most inspiring and challenging time that we've ever shared as friends and as artists. We simply couldn't of imagined connecting with as many people as we have since the release of our debut in 2013.

We have toured the world playing over 25,000 shows in 400 different countries (that's a slight exaggeration but it was a lot) and we have had the privilege of encountering the countless faces that make up our incredibly loyal and ebulliently peculiar fan-base. It is that loyalty that inspired me to write this letter, scrappy as it may be.

This is the beginning of a new chapter for The 1975. Our new record signifies the start of a new world for us, a more colourful world, a less colourful world. We want to play shows, we want a real shared experience, we want to play HUGE shows that we never thought were possible. We want to play sets at festivals that people talk about for ages 'cos it was fun and it was music and the weather was perfect and we want to be honest otherwise what's the fucking point?

So the best way to start is the way we did before – in venues we have loved and places that feel intimate enough to do a proper new show. With people who really want to be there. Or need to be there in some extreme cases.

The venues for the tour were relatively modest in size, making it almost a test of loyalty for fans to see if they were dedicated enough to get a ticket: 'Due to the size of the venues that we feel are appropriate for this particular tour,' said Healy, 'and taking into consideration the humbling [that word again] dedication that I have felt from a lot of our fans I predict that only the most dedicated will end up with tickets. This can only be remedied by our reciprocated dedication to playing more and more shows. I'll see you soon with more music and drama and you've known the title all along.'

The title? Yes, the title. There had been previous hints that the new album would be 'conceptual' in nature. No one was expecting one with quite such a long name: *I Like It When You Sleep For You Are So Beautiful Yet So Unaware Of It*.

It's far from being the longest album name ever – it's fairly succinct compared to the likes of Chumbawamba's 2008 release: *The Boy Bands Have Won, and All the Copyists and the Tribute Bands and the TV Talent Show Producers Have Won, If We Allow Our Culture to Be Shaped by Mimicry, Whether From Lack of Ideas or From Exaggerated Respect. You Should Never Try to Freeze Culture. What You Can Do Is Recycle That Culture. Take Your Older Brother's Hand-Me-Down Jacket and Re-Style It, Re-Fashion It to the Point Where It Becomes Your Own. But Don't Just Regurgitate Creative History, or Hold Art and Music and Literature as Fixed, Untouchable and Kept Under Glass. The People Who Try to 'Guard' Any Particular Form of Music Are, Like the Copyists and Manufactured Bands,*

Doing It the Worst Disservice, Because the Only Thing That You Can Do to Music That Will Damage It Is Not Change It, Not Make It Your Own. Because Then It Dies, Then It's Over, Then It's Done, and the Boy Bands Have Won.

Still, pretty long. Sharp-eyed fans had spotted the title as having been previously used as a photo caption on Healy's Instagram account. Healy said that he'd decided that this was to be the album's title some time back – it was, he explained, something he'd said to a girlfriend at the time. 'There was a time where I was kind of scared about making the next record,' he told *SPIN* magazine. 'The big revelation that I had was that it was all about conviction… I made the decision in that state of mind, that kind of, Right, this is it, I'm doing it. This is the name of the album. I know it's really long, but this is it.'

As for the pink: 'We needed a colour scheme that was just as concise as black and white,' Healy told the *Nothing But Hope And Passion* website, 'so the result is what you see now.'

The act of reinvention echoed the band's skin-shedding changes of name and deletion of material from back in the old days on the Manchester music scene: 'I think they want you to forget the old 1975,' observes journalist Emily Brinnand, who has been keeping tabs on the band since that early piece she wrote in 2012. 'I think they wanted this new image to be projected and wipe out the old monochrome thing. To say, "We're not like that any more, we're this new pink, neon-sign kind of band. It is very interesting to analyse how their image changed. I think a lot of Manchester bands were doing the same style at the same time. Big capital letters with gaps in, monochrome posters, very poetic, very arty. MONEY were doing that, PINS were doing that. The 1975 were also doing that. Whether that was a reason for them to change then… maybe.'

As well as a different look, the band had adopted a different approach to recording the album from first time around, as Adam Hann explained to journalist Tzvi Gluckin: 'After the first album we said we should've gotten together more and played the songs before we recorded them. When we took the first album out on tour, we played the songs night after night and little parts evolved – naturally they get played a certain way that's more comfortable.

'When we did the second album, we wanted to get together and play the songs and ideas we had so that process would happen before we started cutting it. But the studio is an unlimited place of creativity. We weren't going to get bogged down on the idea of, "Oh, we won't do this because it's impossible to do live." We just do what we want to do – what sounds good and is right – and when it comes to playing the show we'll work out how we're going to do it live.

'We've got these creative guitar lines and massive layers of synths and keyboards – we didn't get bogged down on the idea that it can't be done. We'll make it work. There'll be a live version. We just want the recording of the song to be the best it can.'

While recording in Los Angeles Healy managed to get himself

splashed across the *TMZ* gossip website after visiting The Nice Guy nightspot in West Hollywood. Paparazzi video journalists regularly hang around outside the club, but that night word had got out that Healy had managed to get into a row with Justin Bieber, who was at the upmarket celebrity lounge with The 1975 fan Selena Gomez. Healy's boisterous behaviour left Bieber wondering who the curly-haired Englishman was and who the hell had let him in. 'I'm like, Fuck you, Justin Bieber, you little bitch!' Healy told *Rolling Stone*.

When he left the club, Healy got chatting with some fans while waiting for his car. Seeing he was surrounded by cameras, he did the only sensible thing: he started smoking weed from a giant glass bong. 'It's scrummy,' was the Healy verdict. 'Paparazzi?' he scoffed as he took hit after giant hit on the pipe, 'Who's gonna watch this shit? No one cares. I love Los Angeles, it's so much fun. It's better than London – people don't do this in London – people just moan about stuff and eat fish and chips… I am *so* wrecked.'

When Healy finally got to his car, he was asked about the rumoured dust-up with Bieber. 'They're both perfectly normal human beings who are just getting on with their lives,' he said. 'You should do the same.'

Healy soon found himself all over *TMZ* – no one was interested in whether he'd had a row with Justin Bieber any more. The video of him puffing on the bong was there for all to see the following morning: '1975 Singer Matthew Healy – Ripping Bong Hits With Fans On Sidewalk!!' said the headline.

'Really stupid,' an unusually penitent Healy later told *Rolling Stone*. 'I usually never put myself in those situations.'

In autumn 2015, The 1975 watchers got their first chance to hear what the new 'pinker' live sound was like when the band unveiled their new single on Annie Mac's Radio 1 show on 5 October. Never one to make a bold claim when an outrageous one will do, Healy told the presenter that the band wanted nothing less than to be 'ambassadors for this generation'.

'There's a lot lacking in pop music these days,' Healy said. 'It's such an amazing lexicon and vocabulary of sounds... and there's just not enough good bands, man, and I'm sick of it. I'm just sick to death of it. We just want to be like all bands that we have loved before, where you reinvent yourselves but make it feel like a natural evolution.'

Conceding there was an even more glaringly obvious eighties influence on their new music, he added: 'It was a time where pop music wasn't overly encumbered with self-awareness or trying to be too cool. That's why you got amazing bands like INXS or what Bowie was doing at that time.'

Not everyone was convinced that the track was a good move on first hearing it: 'When they released "Love Me", I thought, all their young fans are going to hate this!' Manchester promoter Ben Hiard told me. 'It's like Ian Dury & The Blockheads or something. It's really weird with a theremin effect like something off *Ghostbusters*.' (Weirdly, the theme from *Ghostbusters* was a song the band played at their very first gig.)

'Love Me' had begun as a soundcheck jam and developed into a full-on INXS-meets-Prince strut. But the first comparison that came to many people's minds was: 'David Bowie's "Fame".'

Healy soon got into the habit of asking interviewers what year the Bowie track came out... 1975, he would point out. A joke inside a joke. 'It was [written] at a time when we were on tour all the time and I'm there with my shirt open like messianically giving it to the crowd and I wanted a song that was like, Love me if that's what you wanna do,' the singer explained to music journalist Larry Bartleet. 'It's about a lack of self-awareness. If you're offended by that song you have to admit to being un-self-aware – which none of us are – so we're all mates. The way that I address [our fans] is by giving them the benefit of the doubt and assuming they're in on the joke. Of course I'm taking the piss out of myself for allowing myself to get there.'

Though 'Fame' was the obvious reference with its skinny funk guitar riff, it also seemed to channel Bowie's 'Fashion', particularly in the shape of Hann's convoluted guitar solo. Robert Fripp was responsible for the wall of jagged noise on the Bowie hit – Fripp has also worked with band favourites like Brian Eno, Peter Gabriel, David Sylvian and Daryl Hall.

Hann is particularly proud of the solo, which was achieved by feeding the guitar through a micro-synthesiser: '[We] fired bits of it back out through different pedals, amps, and delays to make this really weird sort of character for the solo,' he told *Premier Guitar*. 'We had a lot of fun recording that. Mike

Crossey, who recorded the album, said it's probably one of the best guitar solos – not so much in terms of the playing on it, but in terms of the creativity behind the whole identity of it, that he's ever recorded. So it was cool.'

The video was directed by the vastly experienced Diane Martel, who has worked with everyone from The Killers to N.E.R.D but needed some convincing to work with The 1975. 'I went to her house,' Healy later revealed to MTV, 'and she said, "I don't really want to make a music video, I don't need to." So I put the idea to her. She has such a great eye for fashionable references.'

The video features model-licking, moonwalking, selfie-drumming and Harry Styles-kissing. It's the all-new 1975 – forget the monochrome, lighten up, everyone, it's just a lark – and Healy is given full rein to prance about with no top on but wearing a whole load of blue eyeshadow.

The first shot in the video to accompany the song is of a pink Jaguar guitar – a Jag is a very 1975 kind of guitar, but the fact that it's pink was the signal that this was the 'new' pink version of the band threatened in the online flyer earlier in the year. The band appear in front of an array of celebrity cardboard cut-outs – from Rita Ora to Ed Sheeran and Harry Styles, via Elvis and Bruce Lee. They had to get permission to use many of the images: 'I texted Rita and said, "Can I put you in the video?" and she said, "Yes, as long as you don't hump me,"' Healy said. 'I humped everything in that video. I'm going around humping and licking, licking everything. Couldn't get in touch with Taylor [Swift], got in touch with Ed, managed to get in touch with Harry. I thought it was going to be easy but it was so boring. People are so boring. They worry about so much stuff.'

Healy gives it the full Michael Hutchence as he rips into the selfie-obsessed culture of fame for fame's sake. Just to drive the idea home, he has his own face printed onto his body – in reference to a famous shot of Richey Edwards of the Manic Street Preachers with Marilyn Monroe's face stamped onto his torso. Narcissm, self-obsession, me, me, me. 'I see all these celebrities all kind of hanging out with one another and I'm very suspicious of whether they're actually friends or not,' Healy told the *NME*. 'As soon as famous people of my generation get near each other – you know who I'm talking about, your Cara Delevingne and Kylie Jenner people – they're all a tight group and I don't really know what they represent. People just want to be in photographed with people. "Squad goals." The phrase makes me die. I'm a musician, not a socialite who ended up in a band. That is my love: music as a form. I'm not doing it because I wanna, I don't know, shag birds or be famous. I'm doing it because it really turns me on. When I have that moment on my own writing, when I get it, I equate it with a sexual desire; it's like a carnal thing within me. It's not about anybody else.'

'By far the poppiest thing the band have ever done – and that's saying something,' said *Gigwise* in their review of the single. 'It's part Red Hot Chili Peppers at their most infectious, but ultimately soaked in a 1980s vibe where "Let's Dance" era Bowie shamelessly meets the sexiest moments of Prince along with the shoulder-padded power pop of Peter Gabriel's "Sledgehammer", with some Bros and 1980s sax thrown in for good measure.'

Billboard also had fun spotting the sheer volume of influences and references in the track: '"Love Me", the first single from British quartet The 1975's second album, is a spirited step away from the radio-friendly teen rock of its debut. An impressive coming-of-age shift, the song sounds like classic Peter Gabriel, while frontman Matthew Healy embraces a newfound rock-star growl.'

Even the band's former enemy, the *NME*, seemed to be coming round to their way of thinking, though the former music weekly firebrand had, by now, been de-fanged after becoming a free paper: 'From the speaker-hopping funky jangle to the unexpected but brilliant cock-rocking guitar solo, "Love Me" fizzes with overweening confidence, fitting for a song Healy says is about narcissism ("got a beautiful face but nothing to say"), and is a monster hit whatever their inspirations. Hang on, Bowie's "Fame"? That's from 1975. They're mucking us about again.'

But it wouldn't be a The 1975 release without it annoying some people, and 'Love Me' was no different. 'It sounds like a bad homage to seventies Bowie and an under-thought, under-inspired plastic pop hit,' said the *Redbrick* website. 'Considering that this is the first single from their upcoming sophomore effort, it doesn't look like The 1975 are going to be turning any heads to their generic, IKEA-flatpack sound. There are a few saving graces from the track, however my most positive thought coming away from "Love Me" was, Hey, wasn't "Fame" a great song?'

As if predicting that the song's irony and references would get up some people's noses, the band put out a statement in a similar hand-typed style to their 'we-are-disappearing' flyer. It was clear that Healy was in no mood for dissent – you're either for us or against us – something he stated in typically flamboyant fashion: 'Too many artists care what others think – we are for the "COMMUNITY"' it read. 'I would die for this, as pretentious or over-reaching as that may sound. I fucking would. This is for the fans.'

But he also had a warning for the critics: if you didn't like the first album, you're *really* going to hate the second one. 'Every criticism, every compliment, every conversation surrounding that first album has been included and been exaggerated,' Healy told *Rolling Stone*. 'Whether it be the accusations of me being like I swallowed a dictionary... There's more emo. The poppier bits are poppier, the eighties bits are eighties-er. It's more like a John Hughes film. It's like a distillation of everything that preceded it, so that's one of the things that I'm really proud of.'

NINE

DOING
A BEATLES

Healy may well have been prepared to die for his music, but his fans were, at the very least, willing to camp outside the students' union building at Liverpool University in the rain to get an up-close look and listen to the band's new sound and altogether pinker look. And that's exactly what they did as The 1975's tour kicked off in November 2015.

Healy would claim that he had been 'shitting it all day' prior to the gig; if that was the case, there wasn't much evidence of it onstage. Supported by Ratboy, The 1975 and their fans were rammed into the far-too-small space that is the Mountford Hall. In a blaze of pink neon they opened up with 'Love Me', rolling out another four new songs along the way: 'Change Of Heart', 'She's American', 'Somebody Else' and 'The Sound'.

The *NME* were there that night. The publication that had

gleefully branded them the worst band of 2014 had certainly changed its tune: 'The new album will take you back to the eighties – or at least if the songs on show tonight are a marker of what's to come,' the paper's Gary Ryan wrote. 'All [the songs] mine an 1980s pop seam that feels more like a calibrated evolution of their sound rather than a revolution. "Change Of Heart" is a soft-focus ballad reminiscent of Madonna's "Crazy For You", with Healy lamenting, *"I just had a change of heart"*. "She's American" raids the bargain bin for the decommissioned sounds of Hue and Cry and Johnny Hates Jazz, all funky guitars, a finger-snapping bridge and a wailing sax solo. It's the kind of guilty pleasure pop you can imagine Alan Partridge introducing by saying something terribly xenophobic.'

Not every reviewer was quite so convinced: 'From the very off, one thing remains clear,' wrote the *Getintothis* website, 'it's all about Matt. Just Matt. On the band come, short hair and black clothes. After a decent amount of "frontman delay" to set the mood, on walks Healy, all long shaggy locks and clad in white linen, almost Christ-like in his self-obsession. Healy preens and swoons at his own sheer bloody wonderfulness at every, and indeed any, opportunity. It's all about him, baby.

'A peculiar set, by an astonishingly popular band, with an obsessive and impressive fan base. They absolutely smashed it, for sure. There is no doubt that the majority of the crowd will remember this night for years to come, we're sure. Maybe it's an age thing, but this correspondent found it all a little soulless and clinically cynical at every turn.'

As the tour continued, another track trailing their album was released – the druggy, self-disgust R&B ballad 'UGH!' Once again, Healy put out a cartoon-strip statement about the song: 'The 1975 are back with a track that's 78 per cent cooler than the last and it's off that album that you can never remember the name of and now it's HERE as an "instant grat"… Maybe it'll get the grown-ups to call us pretentious which I love 'cos bad press isn't even a thing!!!'

By this stage, it was hard to get through an interview with the band without the subject of drugs coming up, particularly their lead singer's enthusiastic consumption of weed. But the cocaine comedown of 'UGH!' seemed almost like a warning. 'I'm not lying – I'm from a white upper-middle-class background from Cheshire, and I've been in a band that's been involved in everything from, like, big festivals to fashion over the past three years,' Healy told journalist Patrick Doyle. 'The social group around me involves cocaine. It does.'

'"UGH!" captures one of the most fascinating facets of The 1975,' said the review in the by now totally 1975-friendly *NME* (indeed, the band was shortlisted in the Best Band category in the magazine's upcoming annual awards). 'Healy's verbose, ostentatious lyrics flying in the face of their position as a band beloved by their fans in the same way as One Direction. It could come across as clunky posturing, the singer trying too hard to prove his intelligence, but, in this track at least, it doesn't sound out of place at all. A song about coming down from cocaine and failed attempts to kick the habit could easily be dreary and self-indulgent. Instead, it sounds practically joyous, bright, supple guitar lines rippling like they're being played on a wobbleboard and a loose rhythm section virtually encouraging finger-clicking, hip-dipping dad-dancing. It's only Healy's lyrics that give way to the darkness at the song's heart.'

The band – and the singer – seemed to have buried the hatchet with the *NME*: 'Well, that's the way the world works,' Healy told the *Nothing But Hope And Passion* website, when asked about his feud with the *NME*. 'People are allowed to change their minds – I think if you go around holding grudges you'll never evolve. I made a career on changing my mind. So if I turned around and told the press they can't do it, I'd be a walking contradiction.'

The video for 'UGH!' – not officially a single – was a disappointingly straightforward affair directed by previous collaborator Adam Powell. It's essentially the band performing in front of their stage set. That's it – high on gloss but low on concept. Not an accusation that could be levelled at the video for the band's official pre-album single, 'The Sound'. It's an overwhelmingly catchy song – like a genetically spliced cross between M People and Maroon 5, all housey piano chords, Motown shimmies, a heavy metal guitar solo and sly wordplay. It even has the word epicurean in it. It has 'hit single' written all over it and it remains The 1975's highest-charting UK song.

'The Sound' would be the album's secret weapon, in a similar vein to their debut's 'Heart Out'. There's a reason for that – the song dates from that earlier period but didn't make it onto their first album. 'I think we just made an album that provided context to that song,' Healy told *Billboard*. 'I think that song is so poppy in its sensibilities, but like everything we do in The 1975 it's juxtaposed to a narrative that's a little more dark or introspective, and I think this album was the perfect vehicle for it. It's the next single in the UK, but we haven't really started with American radio yet for "The Sound". But people really seem to like it when we play it in concert.'

The video for the song sells the viewer a wonderful dummy. The band are seen in a Perspex box with all the usual neon pinkness in place – it looks like we're in for another performance piece like 'UGH!' Then their critics arrive, dressed in white, head to toe; they are the literal opposite to the band as a series of bad reviews are flashed onscreen, at least one of which you might recall from earlier in this book: 'Robotic Huey Lewis tunes', 'Unconvincing emo lyrics', 'Pompous arena synth-pop', 'Genuinely laughable', 'Do people still make music like this?' In the end, the tables are turned and it's the critics who are firmly put in the box. Healy insisted that the video wasn't about getting revenge: 'That was more just referencing the culture that surrounds our band and that divisive conversation,' the singer tried to explain to the *NME*. 'I've not been on some kind of redemption. I'm not about to rise from the ashes. I've never really paid that much attention to what was said about me. I suppose people have the right to their opinions, don't they?'

In the end of 'The Sound' video, The 1975 clearly had the upper hand over the critics. Would that be the case when the second album was finally released? Healy had previously stated that their second album would come out exactly two years after their first – it was five months late in the end, but would it be worth the wait?

As ever Healy was talking the talk right up until its release, claiming he wanted nothing less than artistic acceptance and big sales. 'If you don't want your art to reach people, that negates you as an artist,' he told the *NME*. 'I hate that indie band bullshit of acting like you don't care so you don't get judged about being shit. That's what indie is now. That fey sense of, We don't care. Well, don't do it then. Fuck off and do something else. I'm challenging people to sit through an hour and fifteen minutes and seventeen songs that all sound completely different from each other. It's quite an emotional investment. It's art. It's what I want to do. The world needs this album.'

There would be yet another track released to give people a chance to gauge whether or not they needed the new album – the low-key 'Somebody Else'. As monochrome and downbeat as the previous release had been upbeat and Technicolor, the track is a long and winding affair, something that seemed to put some reviewers off: 'The last single to be released before The 1975 release their new album (entitled *I Like It When You Sleep, For You Are So Beautiful Yet So Unaware of It*, which will surely win longest album title of 2016) is "Somebody Else",' said *The Edge*. 'It's a chilled vibe, quite separate from the pop-like vocals of "The Sound" and a track that allows the vocals of lead singer Matthew Healy to excel. In fact, I really like everything about it – for about three minutes. It's a very long song, and very repetitive.'

'Brash and blinding, The 1975's return has attempted to dazzle at every turn,' pointed out *DIY* magazine. 'Battering its audience over the head with a handbag full of glitter, "Love Me", "UGH!" and "The Sound" have revelled in confusion by cabaret. "Somebody Else" is something different. Gentle and soft-of-touch, it's a slow jam in every sense of the word. Lyrically, Matty Healy finally lays himself bare in the emotional sense, rather than just whipping off his top and skipping about, bottle of plonk in hand and fingers in his ears. At its best, it's captivating. Hauntingly honest, it's a chink-in-the-armour depiction of heartbreak like we've never seen from the band before, a dizzying depiction of that gut-punch moment lost love brings.'

Gig Goer said: 'The track "Somebody Else" is definitely something different from previous releases... Emotionally charged, the song displays deep lyricism having delivered smooth layers and electronic vibes... I mean, you probably noticed that The 1975 like a little bit of showing off. But this gentle approach sees them taking a step further. I've got a feeling that their second record will be so varied that I don't think we're actually ready for what is coming.'

As was becoming the norm, Healy put out an illustrated missive that attempted to explain the thought process involved, though this one was opaque even by his standards: 'This writing should go in your eyes, the plan you see is ADVERTISE! There is a song about myself though it is called "Somebody Else",' it stated. 'You see there is a negative that underlines the positive, for all that I desire to give "The more we consume, the less we live". I know that I may talk too much, just like I'm wired or in a rush, but when it's dark to act like lightning makes it all a bit less frightening: when did they get us believing POP should be devoid of meaning? I know the fans upon this reading will find something worth believing.'

For their manager – who'd stuck with The 1975 for years before anyone was remotely interested – the release of the second album was to be a true taste of his faith: 'The record is amazing,' Jamie Oborne told *Music Business Worldwide*. 'I'm normally hypercritical of stuff I work on but that record is something else. I'm really proud of it. It's the only thing I really listened to for the whole of last year in its various forms and I feel like it sent me a bit mental. There was very real stuff going on while we were making it that related to the record in terms of how emotionally charged it is. Matthew always used to say that he wants to make the soundtrack to people's lives and I found that he made it for our lives as we were living it. It was intense, but a magical thing to share.'

And if Healy's claims about the album seemed far-fetched, Oborne's hopes seemed like science fiction – claiming the band were in a position where they could dominate the charts on both sides of the Atlantic. 'The dream of having a No. 1 album in America and the UK at the same time is what I've been working on for the last four years,' he said. 'Whether or not that's achievable, I don't know. But the most important thing is that the band couldn't have made a better record. There is something really special about the album, for us, as a group of five people, and that already exists.'

As a little primer for what the Americans could expect, the band appeared on legendary US talk show *Saturday Night Live*. Introduced by *Curb Your Enthusiasm* star Larry David – accompanied, rather bizarrely, by US politician Bernie Sanders – they played 'The Sound' and 'Love Me' to a screamy reception from the studio audience. Twitter was ablaze over their appearance, especially Healy's shirtless prancing and preening: 'I wanted to be particularly obnoxious that night. I thought I was being kind of post-ironic and subversive, but it turns out that people in Kansas thought I was an absolute dick.'

After all the talk, bluster, wild claims and pre-released tracks – it had been four months since 'Love Me' had been put out – *I Like It When You Sleep, For You Are So Beautiful Yet So Unaware Of It* was finally released on 26 February 2016. Handsomely housed in a pink and light grey artwork by Samuel Burgess-Johnson it was a beguiling and baffling affair.

The deluxe edition of The 1975's debut album came with a variety of whistles and bells – the previous four EPs, essentially. The band's second album came with all the whistles and bells already attached. *I Like It When You Sleep, For You Are So Beautiful Yet So Unaware Of It* is a pre-loaded, already-deluxed release, a sprawling, unruly, fascinating affair that – like the band themselves in the video for 'The Sound' – refuses to sit neatly and tidily in its predetermined box. Despite Healy's later insistence that he would expect people to cherry-pick tracks, it's a post-iPod album – it shouldn't be for shuffling or playlisting at all; it's for putting a chunk of time aside and wrestling with in one go. It's inconveniently long. That's the way it is. Deal with it.

Actually, the best way to listen to *I Like It When You Sleep, For You Are So Beautiful Yet So Unaware Of It* is on vinyl – it was released on double translucent ice-coloured vinyl in a pink and monochrome gatefold sleeve, no less – as it gives you the opportunity for a break three times when it comes to having to turn it over… Just like they did in the olden days. It even has a cumbersome, wordy title that harks back to the glory days of early eighties Orchestral Manoeuvres in the Dark-style pretension. Let's just call it *ILIWYSFYASBYSUOI* for short, shall we?

A self-titled instrumental kicks things off – a very similar affair to the breathy soundscape that opens their debut, but subtly different. The gentle breathiness is a red herring – we're about to get battered by a tsunami of music. 'Love Me' – with that Bowie riff – keeps things familiar. Little did we know that Bowie would be lost to us a matter of weeks before the album's release. Healy said that the song is about 'a lack of self-awareness', adding, 'I'm making an observation on the glaringly obvious superficial elements that surround my life and the culture that I feed into.'

So, just to be clear: It's a song about fame... that sounds like 'Fame'.

'UGH' jumps us forward in time to the nineties with its funky collection of pops, locks and tiny riffs and jams. Cocaine looks like the thing that's causing the self-disgust of the title. It's taken Healy's money and his sex drive but still he can't say no. In 'A Change of Heart' – a track that was released just days before the album as a last-minute trailer – we find Healy feeling sorry for himself as he toys with splitting up with his girl as his touring life keeps him away from home. What's more, he smells bad too – it's a strange twist on a well-worn theme for second albums: that of moaning about touring, living the life and being a pop star.

The thing that many pop stars seem to moan most about these days is being messed about by Taylor Swift, and Side One rounds off with 'She's American' – a song that appears to be about just that. Indeed, this track and 'A Change of Heart' are both thought to have been inspired by Healy's dealings with La Swift. 'She's American' sees him feeling out of place with his British sensibilities, strange diet and wonky teeth – is he just being used because he's hip? Musically it reeks of the kind of eighties bands that the Brits were great at exporting to the US but that were less popular back home, The Fixx and Wang Chung being particular examples.

'If I Believe You' is the first real shock of the album – a gospel-soaked, crisis-of-faith cry for help, with a trumpet solo by D'Angelo collaborator Roy Hargrove. Healy is an outspoken patron of the British Humanist Association, which promotes living a good, fulfilling life without the aid of religion. Yet here he is calling out for a sign from his maker, just in case he's got it wrong and there really is a God. You don't get that on a One Direction album. 'If I Believe You' completely wrong-footed critics who believed The 1975 were just a synth pop revival band: 'The idea of having genres is on its way out,' Healy explained to music writer Amber Sampson. 'It's certainly not something that I've really been a purist towards. I don't consider ours to be any type of record; it's just *our* record. It's representative of the way the people listen to music now. Gospel music has always been close to my heart, whether it's Ray Charles, Donny Hathaway, traditional gospel or modern gospel musicians who find their way into bands like Stevie Wonder's. We wanted to write a song like that.'

Just in case anyone is worried that Healy has gone all serious and existential on us with his plea to heaven, up next is 'Please Be Naked'. Title-wise at least, order in The 1975-land is restored. It's one of a number of oblique, Eno-esque instrumentals that pepper the album – it would be interesting to isolate them and make them into a mini album of their own. 'Lostmyhead' seems to be heading the same way before a simple two-line lament from Healy breaks up the instrumental vibe before it goes all Sigur Rós at the end.

If *ILIWYSFYASBYSUOI* was a single album, then 'The Ballad of Me and My Brain' – a more Healyesque title it would be difficult to find – would be the final track, coming as it does on the end of Side Two of the vinyl release. Here he seems to be sending up his own self-absorption as he looks for his brain in bars, buses and supermarkets against a backdrop of drones and drums like Toto's 'Africa'.

'Somebody Else' is actually more traditionally ballad-like, akin to the band's beloved brand of Americanised soundtrack music. In it, Healy tells a tale of not wanting his girl anymore, but not wanting anyone else to want her either. The song works far better as an album track than it did as a standalone track and would later lend itself to a marvellously self-serving video. 'Loving Someone' is the accompanying track to 'Love Me', with Healy telling the kids like it is – you deserve better than celebrity crap, be yourselves or follow something or someone that's actually worth following. You can imagine the words printed on a motivation poster, hanging on a wall. Then the title track washes down the decks with an ambient soundscape that's like a chill-out techno version of the *Grey's Anatomy* theme – it's a reminder of their EP days.

Halfway through side three – after the ambient abstraction of the title track – the big guns are unleashed in the shape of 'The Sound'. It's pure cheek to leave the song buried this deep into the album. It's simply a slayer – with multiple hooks and choruses coming at you from several different directions, it's quicker to surrender. Again, we are left wanting more at the end of a 'side' after being given an addictive piece of sugar.

'This Must Be My Dream' has the kind of swing and sheen that used to be found in Jam and Lewis productions in the

1990s, such as The Human League's 'Human' – lyrically it's the most 'normal' song on the album, with very few flights of fanciful wordplay on offer. Next track 'Paris' is a song that has a whiff of familiarity to anyone of a certain age – or anyone, like Healy, with a fascination with the eighties. It's a so-close-it's-a-lawsuit-waiting-to-happen take on Yazoo's 'Only You'; the track was a No. 2 hit in 1982, but Healy claims he came across it after it was used in an episode of Ricky Gervais's TV series *The Office*. 'It's just one of the most classic, perfect, beautiful songs ever,' he later told *Oyster* magazine. 'I wish that was my song.' Well now, in a sense, it *was* his song.

The lightness of tone shown by 'This Must Be My Dream' and 'Paris' lulls us into a very false sense of security before the final two tracks. 'Nana' is just acoustic guitar and the merest of rhythms – a hymn to Healy's late grandmother, who he hopes will live on through people singing along to the song at gigs, rather than through a religious notion of heaven. It could be cloying and awkward – it isn't; it's beautiful. Then, finally, there's 'She Lays Down'– another hymn, this time to his mother Denise and her battle with depression. 'Most people my age, and in my position, probably wouldn't write about the death of their grandmother, or the postnatal depression of their mother – because why would you?' Healy would later tell *Hot Press*, as ever using an interview almost like a therapy session to work through his feelings. 'It's not really appropriate. But that's what I thought was real about this album.'

On 'She Lays Down' we even hear Healy psyching himself

up to deliver the song. He details very specific events in his life – like flying to Australia to visit dad Tim and his mother's use of cocaine – it's the closest thing to a full-on 'diary song' the band have ever done. All whistles and bells are left off this time. Healy is slightly off-mic but it doesn't matter. He's prepared to leave his guts on the recording studio floor and that doesn't need tons of eighties reverb and spot-on recording techniques. You worry that he's not going to make it to the end: he does. 'That was it,' says Healy, and the album is done.

With so many lavish claims made by Healy, plus the sheer amount of music on offer – a double album to all intents and purposes – The 1975 had effectively picked a fight with their critics. They'd made a big, weird, daft, ambient, disco rock record… in fact, just to be extra annoying they'd made *two* of them. 'There were no rules to this record, which is why it's such an eclectic, long record,' Healy told US journalist Joe Lynch. 'The only mission statement was to make sure it was a distillation of anything we'd done before. I wanted to expand the world of the first record. It's a complete evolution and extension, but it also references the first one and jokes about the naiveté of the first one compared to the resignation of the new one. There's so much subtext and Easter eggs, musical references to the last record and lyrical narratives that finish previous songs.'

It's unsurprising that some were perplexed by what the band were up to – the *Guardian* decided it was, 'an album that fancies itself as a challenging work of art, but turns out to be a collection of fantastic pop songs full of interesting, smart lyrics, but also peppered with self-conscious lunges for a gravitas it doesn't really need. Whether that makes it a success or a failure depends on whose metric you use, although there's a sense that, for all his grandstanding, Healy may know where his strengths really lie... its failings aren't going to preclude *I Like It When You Sleep...* becoming a vast success.'

The *NME* was firmly on board though: 'When a band conquers the charts with a fun but inoffensive debut album, you don't expect them to return with a seventeen-track follow-up that tempers pop tunes with swampy post-rock instrumentals and references mental health, religion, addiction, loneliness and fame,' summarised Rhian Daly. 'But The 1975, whose self-titled debut hit No. 1 in 2013, aren't concerned with playing it safe. Frontman Matthew Healy told *NME*, "The world needs this album" and for the most part, he's not wrong. Any record that burrows as deep into your psyche as *I Like It...* should be considered essential. It's hugely clever and wryly funny, too.'

For the Americans, *Rolling Stone* weighed in with a some-what buffoonish review: 'Hey, what gives, fellas? INXS and Duran Duran weren't around in 1975. This ascendant UK quartet ground their second album in sleek dance rock that often feels like it was sculpted on a gaudy eighties budget as the band mates tried hard not to get too sweaty in their aqua-neon sport jackets. The album's rambling, vaguely emo title is a giveaway: despite opening big, bright and airtight, *I Like It When You Sleep...* gets boring-melty during dream-gaze reveries like "Please Be Naked" and "Lostmyhead". Even so, when they hit the right kind of moody sheen ("Somebody Else," "Loving Someone"), The 1975 are an enjoyable balance of desire and distraction.'

But for some, the album was nothing short of a triumph: 'In many ways, if Daft Punk were our generation's Led Zeppelin who drew a year zero line in the sand, then The 1975 are probably the first of the new generation to imbibe all the best bits of the distant and recent past,' said *Drowned In Sound*, 'whilst being cynical enough about the present to re-present it in a way that both fits in (they're very #relevant) and is an anathema to the hits-driven culture from which they are – as the kids say – killin' it. What they've made is a bold body of work that sounds effortless and odd and sophisticated. What they do next is likely to be stadium-filling and bonkers and brilliant, but it matters little when what they're doing now is so sensational.'

Just as the album was released, the band embarked on an audacious five-night run of gigs at London's Brixton Academy. 'This is a big week for us,' Healy warned the crowd. 'We've got a big set for you tonight,' before embarking on a twenty-two-strong selection of songs, nearly half of which were from the new album. Healy would put so much into the opening couple of nights that he needed massage therapy on his neck – 'too much frontman hair-flicking' was his astute self-diagnosis – but he was going to have to pace himself if he was to last the whole run.

The show was essentially an arena production squeezed into a venue whose maximum capacity is 4,900. Some reviewers felt that the scale of the show somewhat overwhelmed the setting: 'That's why we wanted to do that kind of thing – so it felt kind of maximalist and intimate,' Healy tried to explain to the *NME*. 'Is that a word, maximalist? It is now. I wanted it to be like *Close Encounters*, where there's this really imposing presence, like really big thing in front of you that's almost quite alien… We were very strict about wanting it to represent the record. I think that there's so much attention to the detail in the record and so much love in the record, that we wanted it to be powerful really live.'

First night reviewers seemed to agree: 'As they burst through the modern radio classic of "Chocolate" into the immaculate and soulful sheen of "The Sound" and the finale of the bubblegum glee of "Girls",' said *Gigwise*, 'the intimacy of seeing a band so unfathomably huge in a venue like this leaves us in no doubt that five nights at Brixton Academy could have so easily been two nights at The O2 Arena, or more. Make no mistake, they'll get there before you know it because their momentum is unstoppable. We daresay they'll headline Reading or Glastonbury within three years. But for now, the year 2016 well and truly belongs to The 1975.'

'It was quite hard,' admitted Healy to the *NME* partway through the run. 'I've never done a set that long. Physically, it was hard. Emotionally, it was quite cathartic. I felt like I was really, really getting out what I wanted to do onstage.

Obviously there were fears of being slightly indulgent and it is quite a long set, but then again, it speaks of this record. There's a lot of EP stuff on there and a lot of stuff from the new record. I was worried about it being a bit indulgent, but then I realised I'm not indulging. I'm doing it because I know that we need to express who we are as a band and we should do that to our fans. Obviously we're not going to do that at fucking Reading or anything, that'd be mental. But we'll always keep it quite long.'

As the Brixton run of shows hit their stride, it was confirmed that the new album had gone straight in at No. 1 in the UK album charts, selling more copies than nearest rivals Adele and David Bowie combined. 'Thank you so much to everyone involved, we're very, very humbled by it,' Healy told the *Official Chart Show*, as ever using his new, favourite word, 'humbled', as the band were presented with a trophy for making it to the top of the charts. 'We're finding it a bit surreal and weird, we didn't expect it to go to No. 1, we're up against people like Adele, so we're really, really proud. And you get a trophy now, so we feel like we've actually won something too!'

UK music insiders had been predicting the album's No. 1 success since midweek, but there was now another tantalising proposition on the cards as the Brixton shows continued: a simultaneous American No. 1 album. Could they join a select band of acts with a No. 1 on both sides of the Atlantic? Only fifteen bands had managed it previously and the list read like a *Who's Who* of British rock: Led Zeppelin... Rod Stewart...

The Rolling Stones. The first act to manage it were The Beatles in 1964 with *A Hard Day's Night*.

On 7 March 2016 it was revealed that The 1975 had sold nearly 100,000 copies of their second album in America, so adding their name to the hallowed list. What's more, the band bagged themselves another record on the way – that of Longest Ever US No. 1 Album Title, taking the honour from the previous record holder, LL Cool J.

'It is very exciting,' Healy told journalist Rhian Daly. 'It feels very surreal in the truest sense because I can't picture a kid in Kentucky sitting there, listening to the album, so it's still a weird thing for me. It's humbling and I suppose it means that I was right or that the things that I believed in, in the record, did actually translate, which obviously makes me quite proud. I really believed in that record. I suppose what it means is we're definitely part of history now. That's something, isn't it? That's an achievement that came out of nowhere. I don't really know. I think it's… yeah… I mean… yeah. What can I say? It's amazing. No. 1 album in America is a statistic that you hold up to superstars. It's a weird thing to think about and try and understand.'

The news put an added zing into the remaining Brixton shows but – as with the time their debut album went to No. 1 in the UK – the circumstances around finding out the news were somewhat underwhelming. Healy's brother Louis had come to London to spend some time with him and was staying at his home in Hackney. The pair played video games into the early hours before going to bed. Healy only had one duvet and gave it to his fifteen-year-old brother. The only thing available to sleep in was a towel. During the night a text came through from manager Jamie Oborne that *ILIWYSFYASBYSUOI* had gone to No. 1 in the States.

Healy read it – then went back to sleep.

TEN

DRESSED IN WHITE,
HEAD TO TOE

When asked in March 2016 if The 1975 were set to be the biggest band in the world, Healy gave a typically entertaining rely: 'Probably. For a bit. I dunno. Maybe. I know that we have the potential to be. Let's hope? We're giving it a go. We're obviously giving it a go, aren't we?'

In the meantime, there was the small matter of a four-night residency at the Manchester Apollo to deal with, hard on the heels of the Brixton run. Supported by The Japanese House – aka Amber Bain, a musician that Healy and Daniel had been collaborating with – the live show they brought to the Apollo was yet another upgrade on their previous visit. As the number of nights in Manchester increased, so too had the size of the shows and the sheer number of people onstage. At times there were twelve musicians onstage, with extra guitars, sax and a gospel choir. As they were as close to Wilmslow as a band of their popularity could feasibly play, it was treated as a homecoming: 'We're The 1975,' Healy said, 'and as you obviously already know, we're from Manchester.'

Pedantic geography aside, it was clear that the band were easily on track to being the biggest act to come from their adopted home city for a very long time. It was becoming OK to like The 1975: 'Why shouldn't this band appeal to everybody?' said writer Joe Goggins in his review for music website *The Line of Best Fit*. 'They've an embarrassment of hooks and melodies that should endear them to the alternative crowd, and an unfailingly sharp ear for the electronic affectations that currently dominate the mainstream. And then, on top of that, there's Healy, the consummate frontman, all Jaggeresque arrogance, the omnipresent glass of red in one hand and the crowd in the palm of the other. It is frankly bizarre that this ragtag pop outfit are so obviously bound for arenas before the year's out, but here we are. The 1975 continue to stake their claim for the latest slot in a pantheon of great British pop weirdos, and sure enough, it's the country – not just their hometown – that should be taking them to its collective heart. On current evidence, we're getting there.'

While he was near home, Healy proved that he was game for most things when he agreed to take part in the 'School Run' feature on the Radio 1 breakfast show. It was a return to his old stomping ground as the singer drove three pupils to Cheadle Hulme School for the benefit of Nick Grimshaw's listeners.

Pupils Holly, Eleri and Harrison fired questions at Healy – whose accent immediately reverted to full Cheshire – as he drove them through the country lanes. He was asked about his first kiss, fancying Coldplay singer Chris Martin, and even rapped 'Ignition' by R. Kelly. 'It was a huge surprise, our school told us we were going on a wellbeing trip so we wondered what was going on when Nick Grimshaw showed up!' Eleri told her school's website. 'It was nice to get to know Matty; we talked about school in general, his childhood, sexuality and all sorts of other things. I really enjoyed it. It was the talk of the school!'

Healy was charm itself until the pupils got out of the car to go into school. After bidding them a cheery farewell, he turned to Grimshaw and said: 'I hate kids…'

Meanwhile, something was happening in terms of the way The 1975 were being perceived by the music media. The band's second album was shifting them on to the radar of the more 'grown-up' critics and their more grown-up readers. The serious monthly magazines – not all of whom fully appreciated the band – seemed to smell the wind and get on board with The 1975. The doyen of such publications, Q magazine, even put the band on their front cover, under the headline: 'A Band To Blow Your Mind'. It's perhaps telling that Q had understood *ILIWYSFYASBYSUOI*. The magazine launched in 1986 and many of the acts that The 1975 used as reference points had graced the cover over the years. 'As ambitious an album as you will hear from a young British group and they mostly pull it off,' was Q's view of the band's second album.

There seemed to be all sorts of reasons why *ILIWYSFYAS-BYSUOI* should be a success, yet there it was, top of the charts on both sides of the Atlantic. Healy listed the reasons why it shouldn't have achieved this feat in an interview with the *NME*: 'It's got a weird title, it's particularly long, it's from a band that hasn't had much chart success from their singles.'

He went on: 'It's not on paper something that a lot of people would run away from, but I think it's a testament to how I feel we put so much love into it and I really have been feeling so much love coming back from it in a way that I've never really felt before. I feel really understood for the first time. I feel like I've had a career of being quite misunderstood. That record is really drenched in my identity, it's kind of everything that I am. So for it to be so accepted makes me feel quite accepted.

'I just don't want to provoke ambivalence in people. That's like the worst thing that you can do. I think there's a lot of bands that do that, whether that's through playing it safe or just not being good enough.'

Meanwhile, many interviewers had been asking Healy how long the band could avoid moving up to arena level – it seemed like they were avoiding the inevitable. On 22 March the inevitable happened and the band stepped up to the plate, playing the Birmingham Arena, their biggest ever show.

'Now we're an arena band – that's what band we are,' admitted Healy to journalist Aidin Vaziri. '[Birmingham] was a good show, but when I came off the stage, I was like, Fuck this! I need to be really engaged. I need to be able to really, really give myself. I didn't like it at all. [But] I realised we can do an arena now because we played all those small rooms. It's not radio fans with their mum. Now when we play an arena, it's loads of weird kids who love our band. No matter how big it gets, as long as we keep addressing those kids, everybody is in the gang.'

Among the crowd in Birmingham was Manchester DJ Dan Deighan, who'd watched the band from their days as Drive Like I Do nearly a decade earlier: 'I went to watch them at Birmingham Arena. I felt like I had to. I'd seen them play to twenty people and watched them get bigger and bigger. It was incredible to see it go full circle. I got a proud feeling that I'd seen this grow from such a small seed to this huge thing.'

In May 'Change of Heart' became the latest song from the album to get a video treatment. The down-tempo ballad that may or may not be about Taylor Swift was accompanied by an equally low-key set of visuals. Out went the pink neon and the mocking self-depreciation; back in came the black-and-white moodiness. Healy was the sole representative of the group to be seen in the promo, performing a Chaplinesque dance routine that had echoes of Ed Sheeran's 'Thinking Out Loud', only with Michael Jackson moves and a Madonna 'Crazy For You' vibe thrown in for good measure. 'I want to convey the sense of resignation in being a clown,' Healy said in his usual lengthy explanation. 'I am, have been and will always be a clown. I think it can tire people. For the sake of subtext and self-reference it should be black and white. Also more chic.'

For someone who says he has no interest in acting, Healy

makes a pretty decent fist of portraying the lovelorn mime artist, but the song and the video treatment left the band wide open to attack from critics, with some, like Timothy Gabriele of *PopMatters* practically taking a run-up before sticking the boot in: 'This is dreadfully dull. It's Ultravox after Foxx left, the Human League after they sold out, and OMD when they were sick and tired of seeing everybody else get theirs and decided to cash in. But at least those defeated groups had the good sense to not put a dying cat solo square in the middle of their drafted-in-rhythm-with-a-John-Hughes-montage artless shamwow. This is retro for people weaned on the travesty of what passes for remembrance on the pop stations these days. Yacht rock without chillwave's innocence bereavement and detourned aesthetic irony. Jesus Christ, there's even a black and white music video featuring mimes. Mimes, for chrissakes! Who is the target audience for this? Hospice patients who grew up in the eighties or actual young people? How much Thorazine is the generation taking?'

It would be drummer George Daniel who'd be in need of medication a few weeks later when the band returned to America for yet more dates. After a show in Kansas the band headed back to their tour bus – drinks were taken and in the early hours of the morning, Daniel managed to fall off the bus, breaking his shoulder. Within a matter of hours, Healy was tweeting the news: 'BAD NEWS: George has broken his shoulder BAD NEWS: He can't play shows for a bit GOOD NEWS: We're not gonna cancel shows'.

The following night the band were back onstage in Tulsa with The Japanese House's Freddy Sheed behind the kit. Healy explained what had happened to the crowd: 'It was one o'clock in the morning. Everyone had had a little bit of a drink – no one's proper pissed. The wonderful George – who isn't sat at the drums, unfortunately – fucking fell off the bus and broke his shoulder. It's 1am, the night before this show, George has got a broken shoulder and we're completely fucked. We were gonna have to cancel the show and then Freddy stepped up to the plate. Freddy's a good mate of ours and plays with The Japanese House; he's not been to bed, he's learned our entire set in one fucking night. He's fucking amazing!'

Barely a week after the band settled down with a more permanent replacement drummer in the shape of Dave Elitch of The Mars Volta, Healy got the news that his dad Tim had been taken ill on the set of his TV show, *Benidorm*. Some tabloids reported that Healy senior was 'fighting for his life' and had been airlifted from the show's Spanish location to Manchester. This was thankfully downgraded to a somewhat less dire prognosis – he was later written out of the series while he recovered.

Meanwhile, despite the fact that he was on the other side of the world – on his way to Canada, in fact, as their North American tour continued – Healy managed to get himself embroiled in a bizarre row over the upcoming vote on whether Britain should leave the European Union. The singer noticed a similarity between the neon album artwork for *ILIWYSFYASBYSUOI* and an ad campaign produced by the Electoral Commission aimed at encouraging young people to vote in the upcoming EU referendum. 'LOOK OUT KIDZ THE GOVERNMENT ARE STEALING OUR THOUGHTS!!' Healy tweeted, even suggesting he wanted to sue the UK Government – perhaps not realising that the Electoral Commission wasn't actually them.

The singer's remarks were relatively diplomatic compared to those of 1975 manager Jamie Oborne: 'What the actual fuck?!?!' he tweeted, with a link to the campaign adverts showing pink neon signs strategically placed around the UK. Just to add extra fun to the row, it was revealed that the person who had shot the campaign photos and video was in fact director Nadia Marquard Otzen, the person behind the band's 'Settle Down' video in 2014.

Oh – and when was the last time there was a referendum on this subject? Why, 1975, of course.

The band could hardly claim to have copyrighted the style – a glance at the billboard and the light poems of conceptual artist Robert Montgomery would dissuade you of that notion – but the similarity was striking. But the idea that something dodgy was afoot took hold to such an extent that the Electoral Commission was forced to put out a statement, denying the band's style and artwork had been appropriated to appeal to the young: 'The visuals of the campaign are designed to "cut through" the noise that everyone will be hearing about the E.U. referendum by creating eye-catching advertising "you can't miss". The visual aspect is based on a successful campaign the

Commission ran ahead of the Scottish referendum where by polling day, 84 per cent of people surveyed said they recognised the advertising.'

Healy would soon have another chance to weigh in with his thoughts on the EU referendum – this time in an even more unlikely situation. On Saturday, 25 June, the band returned to the Glastonbury Festival to play The Other Stage. Top of the bill on that stage were none other than one of the bands The 1975 were constantly being asked about – New Order. Healy favourites Sigur Rós were playing the festival that year, too.

'You've got to bring your A game – it's Glastonbury, everybody's watching,' Healy told the BBC prior to the show. 'And at a time like now as well, this country needs something like this right now – a sense of community and loving each other and getting along. Glastonbury feels even more important.'

Healy's mention of 'a time like this' was telling: the previous day the UK had voted to leave the EU and emotions were still very raw across the country, with many – particularly the young – feeling like they had been betrayed. Dressed in a horrific white flared safari suit, Healy sang, danced and mugged his heart out as the set got underway with 'Love Me'. But, as he'd hinted during his chat with the BBC before going onstage, there was something on his mind. Plus he'd been drinking margaritas.

There were plenty of examples of more 'serious' artists on the Glastonbury bill that year who spoke out about Brexit – Damon Albarn and Billy Bragg, amongst others – but it fell to a young man dressed in a horrible white suit to really sum up the mood. 'This song is about compassion and loving people,' Healy told the crowd. 'I feel like as a young person I've got a responsibility to say something. I mean, what do I know? I don't know fucking anything, I'm a pop star. In a suit. But what I feel – and I know, what a lot of people my age [also] feel – is that there's this sentiment of anti-compassion that's spread across an older generation and voted in a future that we don't fuckin' want. I know, I'm a popstar. What do I know? But it is appropriate for me to say that because I'm here, because we're at Glastonbury – and Glastonbury stands for fuckin' everything that our generation fuckin' wants. Equality. Compassion. Social responsibility. Unity. Community. Everything like that. Fucking *loving* people. I think that when you stand on a stage like this in front of so many obviously beautiful, liberal, intelligent people, it's difficult to say nothing. I love you, Glastonbury.'

The 1975 then played an impassioned, chest-beating version of 'Loving Someone'. It was a bold, political move – only slightly spoilt by the sight of comedy actor and chat-show host James Corden grooving to the band's set at the side of the stage.

Reviewers were, for once, in agreement that The 1975 had been the hit of the day: 'The 1975's breezy, lightweight pop turned out to be a very good fit for The Other Stage at dinner time,' said *The Telegraph*. 'Couples of all ages were dancing, arms clasped around each other, middle-aged men were forcing their teenage daughters to take selfies with them. A double rainbow spread across the whole site. It was all rather lovely, really. And credit to Healy, who did what plenty of other millennial performers have failed to do at Glastonbury this weekend and properly stand up for his generation in the wake of Brexit.'

But *The Telegraph's* review seemed quite guarded in its praise compared to the one filed by *Gigwise*: 'When you dissect the trajectory of most British bands of the last thirty years, a certain performance at Glastonbury will always stand out as a pivotal moment. With such a diverse crowd and so many variables, it basically has the potential to be a career-defining performance for a band, something that pushes them to new heights and wins over a whole different audience. This was that performance for The 1975.

'From their fearlessness to push the boundaries of pop music, to the meticulous craft that goes into their visuals and live shows through to their willingness to speak their mind and ruffle feathers, The 1975 are basically what the world needs right now. Just watch them take over the Pyramid Stage before this decade is out.'

But the most glowing account of the day was surely handed in by the *NME*, claiming that the band's 'knockout performance proved Matthew Healy is Britain's greatest new popstar'.

'The 1975 have just delivered a flawless set comprising mainly of their second album, *I Like It When You Sleep, For You Are So Beautiful Yet So Unaware Of It*,' gushed the magazine's

Larry Bartlett. 'In January, before the album's release they told *NME* that the world "needed" it. It turns out what the world needs are the Manchester guys themselves. In a month where some musicians refused to align themselves with either side of the referendum debate but cancelled concert appearances they later realised had been organised by *Leave.EU*, it's utterly refreshing to have a popstar be so vocal, and here Healy made the most of his platform.'

The 1975's rehabilitation from their previous position as the *NME*'s worst band was clearly now complete. To bolster this idea, their status as an arena act was now not up for discussion either. They'd sold out a show at London's 02 Arena in a couple of hours. This was then expanded into a full-on UK arena tour that would include a second night in London, promising 'expanded visuals and a brand new setlist, including songs that have never been played live. The 1975's constantly evolving performance will fuse art and technology to create a unique live experience.'

The 1975 had gone to another level – even Healy's mum was struggling to get her head around his success: 'When he sells out The O2 [Arena] in three hours, I'm like, "I can't believe you came out of me!"' Denise Welch told *Good Morning Britain* when asked about the band's success, admitting that she now found it difficult to get in touch with her son. 'I text him and don't get much back. I phone his security, Mark, and find out what they're doing.'

One thing Healy had been doing was filming the

elongated art-house video for 'Somebody Else', the Michael McDonaldesque smoocher from their second album. The husky-voiced McDonald – former singer with The Doobie Brothers – had clearly caught the band's ear. 'We're totally into Michael McDonald – we can't stop listening to him,' Healy told FUN 107.1, while demonstrating that he was able to do a pretty reasonable impression of McDonald's strangulated singing style. 'We laugh when we're listening because it's so ridiculous. I don't care about the rules of music and what you're allowed to like anymore.'

'Somebody Else' had been originally put out as a teaser track for *ILIWYSFYASBYSUOI*, but now it was getting the full video treatment, thanks to director Tim Mattia. Right from the start of the video there are self-references to scenes, characters and props from previous promos designed to make fans scurry to the Internet to re-examine the older films. Again, it's all about Healy, and once he's removed his clown make-up from the previous video, he gives his best performance yet as the messed-up protagonist of an urban nightmare. The climax – literally – sees a drugged-up Healy getting hot and steamy in the back of a car… with himself. 'Having sex with myself is quite interesting,' he told Radio 1's *Newsbeat*. 'I had to shoot a love scene with a guy dressed as me. It's 2016, there are no fears about that, but it was an intense creative process. It was a collaboration between me and Tim [Mattia] and it was surreal. We had to shoot almost two or three videos because it goes back on itself.'

Again, Healy and the band were laying themselves wide open to their critics: the ultimate narcissistic singer in the ultimate act of self-loving narcissism. But if you get to make fun of yourself before anyone else can, it takes the wind out of critics' sails. 'Everything that we do could be perceived as pretentious,' Healy told MTV. 'Usually it's just used as a vehicle to talk about what people don't like about me, isn't it? But what I don't do is patronise our fans – or let's just say people. I don't ask for permission, and I give people the benefit of the doubt. Because people are smart. Stupid people are stupid, but there's enough smart people in the world. I like the divisiveness of my band, to be honest with you. The idea of provoking ambivalence in somebody really scares me.'

The fact that the band were self-referencing by planting hidden messages and 'Easter eggs' in their music and videos to be researched and discovered increased the sense of fascination and loyalty between The 1975 and their audience, with Healy very much in the role as Pied Piper-in-chief. 'I want every kid to be able to meet us. I want every kid to have that feeling of, you know, when it's *your* band? I want every kid to have that feeling be justified and not feel like, Oh, they're everyone's band. We are everyone's band, but we're also specifically *your* band.'

But that idea of closeness between artist and public would be tested to breaking point after an incident in America. On 10 June that year the singer Christina Grimmie – a former contestant on the US version of *The Voice* – had been shot dead by an obsessed fan at an after-show meet-and-greet session in Orlando, Florida. The gunman, Kevin Loibl, shot himself after being tackled by Grimmie's brother. Loibl had travelled to the event armed with two handguns, extra ammo and a hunting knife. The incident sent shockwaves through the music community in the US, with Selena Gomez cancelling a Florida meet-and-greet scheduled for the following night after hearing the news. The 1975 were due to start a run of half a dozen North American dates two days after the incident.

Though many musicians had taken to Twitter to express their shock at what had happened, it took Healy to weigh into the issue with both feet when asked if the shooting had changed his notion of meeting and greeting fans: 'I'm not doing it anymore in America – I don't want to do it until something changes,' he told the somewhat ironically named Fun 107.1 radio station. 'And I know nothing is going to change. It's difficult being a British person talking about another country… You don't have a right to talk about it. I totally get that. But as a totally objective thing as a human being, it's like you [Americans] have these two birth defects: institutionalised racism and guns. They're so heavily ingrained in society – you have black people being murdered on streets named after Confederate generals… and you've got people who'd rather see toddlers shot in the head than give over their guns. When a young pop star goes out and gets shot, what am I supposed to think? Is it a legitimate fear of mine to be scared of that? I think it is. It's not about ego, it's not me thinking I'm fucking John Lennon; this girl was a kid from *The Voice*… It's a weird time and people are scared to talk about it. I am [scared to talk about it]… but I'll do it anyway.'

It was another example of Healy being a godsend to journalists – put a microphone near him and he's almost certain to say something newsworthy.

Back home, the summer festival season continued with the band criss-crossing the world to play to huge audiences in Norway, Finland, Spain, Australia, Malaysia, the Philippines, Indonesia and Japan – though they did postpone a series of South American dates due to 'scheduling' issues. The worldwide festival run was followed by a return to Britain and a key appearance at the Reading Festival. The 1975 headlined the *NME*/Radio 1 stage, with the *NME* claiming they 'may just be the best band in the country right now'.

Under the headline 'Fuck The Rest, The 1975 Just Won Reading', the magazine raved about the band's performance: 'From the very start (the irresistible "Love Me") there are fans crying, and the screams that greet the band are deafening. Healy doesn't have to do anything to elicit such a response. When he stands at the front of the stage smoking a cigarette, he gets almost as big a reaction as some of the songs on the setlist. "This is such an incredible experience," he says after "Change Of Heart", "thank you so much." By the time "The Sound" comes round, Reading is a mass of grinning, weeping people. Those who weren't fussed by the band beforehand are converts, united in their newfound adoration in the most euphoric band of the weekend. As the anthemic track reaches its breakdown, Healy instructs the crowd to jump on the count of four. Practically everyone crammed under the canvas obeys his command and it's a beautiful sight.'

At the end of a hit-packed, hour-long set, before finishing with 'Sex', Healy addressed the crowd: 'I don't know what the future holds, but I can promise you two things… One: we're gonna go away and make another record. Two: we're gonna come back and we're gonna fucking headline Reading, I fucking promise you.'

The music press got very excited about the prospect of the band dipping out of view to make another album so quickly – the singer would backtrack slightly afterwards: 'I was pissed out my head,' Healy later confessed to music journalist Luke Morgan Britton. 'Absolutely pissed and talking shit. We are gonna make another record. We never stopped. What I've realised, even for the second album, we never stopped. We're always making music, that's what we do. We will make another record and it will probably happen in a similar way to how we made the last one. We'll just kind of curate it over the next couple of years, or the next year or so and then put something out.'

He didn't back down on the claim that they'd headline Reading though, did he?

Meanwhile, the band's undeniable commercial success was rewarded with a nomination for a Mercury Music Prize, the annual argument-starting shindig to decide on who had arranged the best series of noises and notes and collated them into an album. The list of twelve acts was a very The 1975-friendly affair, with the band sharing the same page as Radiohead, Savages and the late David Bowie.

At an event to announce the nominations, when asked what he'd do with the £25,000 prize money, Healy said he'd give it to charity. 'I mean, we're at a music competition, so that's kind of silly in its essence, so you can't get too worked up about anything like that,' he told reporters. 'The fact that everybody else likes it [the album] is good for them. We've had a lot of fun making it.'

When the final announcement was made, the band were beaten to the award by grime artist Skepta. Healy took the loss in good sprit, tweeting, 'YES ? @Skepta you really are an inspiration!! ?@MercuryPrize thank you so much for everything & awarding the album that truly represents 2016!!'

By that stage, Healy had changed his tune somewhat about what he would have done with the prize money, claiming he would have spent the cash on, 'Just drugs. Endless, endless drugs. All of them! I don't care. Anything that you can sort me out, I'll have that.' Still, the band put on a spirited performance on the night of the televised ceremony, with Healy performing part of 'Love Me' while dancing on a table.

All in all, a very Healyesque night all round.

By now, a fearsome slab of live dates had been put into the band's calendar. As well as their UK arena tour there was to be huge tour of North America, a trek across continental Europe as well as rescheduled dates in South America. The itinerary stretched well into 2017.

Although many of these gigs would be bigger, it's unlikely that any of them would reach the sheer over-the-top grandeur of The 1975's performance at Blackpool's Tower Ballroom at the end of September. The band had agreed to stage a show to mark the end of a month of performances for Radio 1's Live Lounge. They'd decided to make a splash by performing with the BBC Philharmonic Orchestra at the ornate Tower Ballroom. On the run-up to the show, they returned to Manchester to rehearse with the orchestra and conductor Richard Davies – a daunting prospect: 'There were eighty of us in the room when we were rehearsing,' Healy told Greg James of Radio 1. 'They are proper musicians. They are full-on legit. They know what they're doing. When you hear your music played… it's actually really emotional. I got a bit teary at times. It's the way we wanted to celebrate this record and what we've achieved and what we are proud of.'

To reflect the seriousness of the occasion that night in Blackpool, Healy walked out onstage that night in his glasses – though this was slightly undermined by the fact that he was also sporting Rupert Bear trousers and a crimped hairdo seemingly modelled on Sideshow Bob from *The Simpsons*. 'Now this is what I *call* a gig,' Healy told the crowd. Bent over their keyboards and sample pads like a Cheshire Kraftwerk, the band excelled when it came to glacial, ambient tracks, like the title track of *ILIWYSFYASBYSUOI* and 'Please Me Naked'

– with the effect slightly spoiled by superfluous One Direction and Justin Bieber covers. There were even some boos at the mention of Bieber's name: 'Leave him alone,' Healy chided.

The singer was on his best behaviour – the usual sloshed-on-red-wine routine was left behind as Healy swayed with pleasure while the orchestra lifted the songs to a different place. He even started to cry during John Waugh's 'If I Believe You' sax solo. But he seemed happiest during the ambient pieces, air-conducting the orchestra, lost in the music as the sound of the orchestra and his band weaved in and out of each other, building to a cinematic crescendo.

Perhaps Healy was so happy because he finally had what he'd always wanted: a soundtrack – like the John Hughes scores he'd listened to so intently in the past. But this soundtrack was all his own.

ELEVEN

THE BEST SHOW
WE'VE EVER PLAYED

By the autumn of 2016, the statistics swirling around The 1975 were becoming very intimidating indeed to rival bands: over the coming months they were set to play more than 60 shows in 23 countries to a million people. 'We're a very important band now,' Healy told *The Big Issue* with his patented brand of guileless self-confidence. 'I believe that.' And as ever, the singer was utterly unrepentant about his hunger for success and his disdain for indie street cred: 'Playing to 10,000 screaming young women who hang on your every word and live their lives soundtracked by your music or a bunch of crusty north London liberals? I'm telling you, anybody would pick that [the first option]. Because it fucking means something to them.'

Credibility may have been low on Healy's list of priorities, but he was to get it anyway in the shape of a slew of nominations in that year's *Q* magazine awards. The 1975 topped the nominations list – along with Coldplay – with four nods, including the most prestigious award, that of Best Album. The music industry was still recovering from the death of David Bowie at the start of the year, so it was a shock to all concerned when The 1975 beat Bowie's *Blackstar* – the out and out favourite – to win the Best Album award. A shock to everyone, that is, apart from Matthew Healy. The band were on tour in North America so they couldn't collect it in person. Instead, the singer sent a very Healy-esque video message to accept the award; it saw him make his acceptance speech as he crowd-surfed across a sea of young women: 'Thank you for our award,' he said. 'We are the best band with the best album. Isn't that right everybody? We should have won the Best Band also but… only the album. Thank you.'

Another key publication would also make *ILIWYSFYASBYSUOI* its album of the year – the formerly 1975-hating *NME*. 'Any album with a title this unwieldy inevitably opens itself up to ridicule, but it turns out that The 1975 thrive on the ridiculous,' the weekly magazine stated. 'At 74 minutes long, with 17 tracks spanning everything from pop to post-rock and all points in between, the Manchester group's second album was a fascinating reflection of their frontman Matthew Healy's outsized, often contrarian, personality: egomaniacal but introverted, populist but unapologetically pretentious, insecure but hungry for attention. "The world needs this album," Healy told *NME*, and the world's response to it – topping the charts on both sides of the Atlantic – proved him right.'

Despite the plaudits, Healy couldn't resist a sly dig at the publication's previously sniffy attitude towards them: 'Yeah it feels good,' he said. 'But it's a bit like "*so-rrreee*" isn't it? For that time you called us the worst band in the world. My life had changed and I couldn't make another record about being a bored, middle-class teenager in Macclesfield, but I also didn't want to get caught in the trap of making a record about "poor famous me". You know, "Oh God, Champagne tastes horrible; aren't threesomes hard?" So I went quite inward – it's not about going partying, it's an odyssey into my brain.' The *NME* was, by now, so supportive of the band, it devoted a sizable section of an article about the newly-announced Grammy Award nominations to bemoan the fact that The 1975 hadn't received one. 'Despite their new record topping the charts in both the UK and US, as well as picking up our own Album of the Year award, The 1975 are suspiciously absent from any of the categories. Maybe the judges were confused by their name. Perhaps they were offended by "She's American". We just don't know.'

Maybe the *NME* staffer should have read the nominations list properly as the band had in fact been nominated for a Grammy, albeit an unusual one. Healy's keen visual sense rather than his music had caught the judges' collective eye. The band's pink-neon-in-unusual-locations theme for their second album had bagged Healy and designer Samuel Burgess-Johnson a nomination for Best Box Set or Special Limited Edition Package. The pair would be up against releases by Paul McCartney and the late Edith Piaf. Not a Grammy nomination for music – but a Grammy nomination nonetheless. 'Sam's my best mate,' Healy told journalist Dan Stubbs. 'Everything is my idea and then Sam takes it and turns it into whatever. I consider him kind of like my art director, but I would never say that... but I just did. He's a really good mate and he's just a very, very talented guy. I think, because the ideas we had for the visual aspect of the record were quite succinct, it was easy – it was just choosing cool locations. '

The band would also bag a BBC Music Awards gong for their symphonic Live Lounge cover of One Direction's 'What Makes You Beautiful' at their recent Blackpool show. The 90-minute primetime event was broadcast live on BBC1, with The 1975 opening up proceedings with a full-on rendering of 'The Sound'. Healy – sporting a leather jacket, a bow tie and the most appalling pair of shoes ever seen on British TV – even managed to get the awards-show crowd jumping, not an easy task at an industry event. Beating the likes of Craig David and Usher, the band was presented with the award by 1980s pop crooner and fellow Cheshire lad Rick Astley, something that Healy clearly got a kick out of: 'Rick Astley – legend!' he informed the crowd. 'We didn't write it [the song] so we can't take too much credit. But if I'm being really honest and sincere, I want to thank Radio 1 for everything, basically. They've been intrinsic to our success – the Live Lounge and stuff like that – we're so very humbled. Thank you so much.'

Despite his polite acceptance and the usual mention of being humbled, Healy seemed to have a slightly complex relationship with the notion of turning music into a prize-giving ceremony: 'I don't give a fuck about awards; I just want to make records,' he told *Billboard*. 'I'm going to be a pop outsider, don't include me in anything. Oh, Mercury nomination, that does feel quite nice. Maybe I do care about these things. I live these records. I do a show, go to a hotel room, work on music and document my psyche. But it makes me think, if somebody does put as much heart into what they do as we did with that record, then it should be commercially successful. So, I have been a bit surprised, but I have been a bit, "Yeah, too fucking right", too. I worked really hard and I can tell that song connects with people. What I've done now is start to accept the fact that The 1975 is more accepted in different worlds.'

As usual, there was a lot on Healy's mind as 2016 drew to a close – especially after spending so much time in America. They'd slogged their way across the country playing show after show. They were in New York when Donald Trump beat Hillary Clinton to be the next President of the United States – Healy says that he cried when he heard the news. 'I was tired and we felt a bit defeated,' he told the NME. 'I got very much caught up in the race, bigotry, Donald-Trump-says-stupid-things stuff, so when it happened I was like, *Fucking white people, what the fuck are we doing*, you know? But the fact of the matter is America voted for Trump – white, black, Latino, middle class, poor – so the thing now is to understand their genuine concerns. Every night on stage, whether we'd been in a Trump state or not, I'd been saying, "We're English and we know what it's like to fuck up your country very swiftly." And even after I said it, it still happened. Can you believe that?' Healy probably had his tongue squarely in his cheek there – even he wouldn't claim to be able to influence the US elections… could he? 'My band is starting to become a very, very big band – a very important band to lots of young people who have just felt directly disenfranchised by this situation,' he told *NPR Music*. As far as Healy was concerned, it was now part of his job – along with singing, shimmying and waving a glass of red wine about – to be vocal about social and political issues during his performances and, if needs be, on record too: 'We're talking about Brexit, we're talking about the Trump presidency. And the fact of the matter is …my responsibility was always artistic and it was kind of to myself. But now I know that my next record is going to come out within the Trump presidency. I think there's more of an expectancy for art to be more actively challenging what we see every day. And what would be interesting for me is to see how we incorporate that into the way that The 1975 works because The 1975 is kind of like my diary. I'm either really, really frank or it's kind of conversational. When it gets political, it's still all about me. So I don't yet know how I'd make a kind of a record with a punk lyrical ethos.'

After the band delivered the last of their US dates – ending up with three shows in Florida – they announced they'd be opening up pop-up shops in three cities prior to their British arena shows. Three cities were chosen – Los Angeles, London and Manchester – with the 'hometown' event taking place at the Artzu Gallery. It would have been a familiar location to Healy – the gallery is on the site of the old Granada TV studios, where his mum used to work on *Coronation Street*. As well as selling merchandise, the shops also exhibited artwork. The idea that The 1975 were now taste makers in the world of art was something that clearly set off Matthew Healy's 'Warning: Pretentiousness Ahead' alarm: 'I wince at the idea of anybody assuming that I think I'm being educational, whether it be with my music or art,' he told journlaist Rhian Day at the London event. 'This just comes from my love of what I do. I'm not having a case of serious artist syndrome. I'm not doing that. I love the things that I love and this for me matches exactly what I do. I want it to be the visual representation of our music. I think that there is an element of it, with our live show and stuff like that. I wanted it to be like an art installation. I wanted it to feel like a light installation. Because I know who I am and I understand where we sit culturally, I know that there's going to be a lot of our audience who aren't into fine art or aren't into these kind of things. So I suppose there is that element of doing this kind of thing for the masses and immersing people in those ideas, and that's nice, but I don't think, *Oh they need educating* or, *I need to reference this or that.*'

2016 – an extraordinary year for The 1975 – was nearly over. Most bands would look back and pat themselves on the back. As usual, Healy had the future in his sights. And as ever, he had it all planned out: 'We'll put something out next year, whether it be a single or an EP,' he told the *NME*. [New] album in 2018, headline Reading and Leeds that year, headline Glastonbury the year after or the year after that. I mean, I haven't got the offers yet. But I tell you now, I'm doing it. Who else is going to do it?'

In December, weighed down with awards and expectation, is was time for The 1975 to walk the walk as well as talk the talk. Yet regardless of how convincing Matthew Healy's brand of talk could be, there was the small matter of their pre-Christmas tour to deal with. Could they step up and become the arena act they always seemed to have thought they could be? The huge act they always acted like, no matter how small the venue? It was time to find out.

* * *

It's Tuesday 13 December 2016 and The 1975 have just about sold out the Manchester Arena – the largest indoor venue in Europe. The air is damp with the perfumes of both sexes and there is a top note of marijuana seeping its sweet-scented way from the ladies' toilets. The venue is teeming with young couples, indie rockers of indeterminate age, teenage girls and yes-you-can-go-but-I'm-coming-too dads. 'Multiply 30 quid by all the people here...' says a grumpily-impressed parent sitting behind me as he scans the crowd. 'That's a lot of money.'

Having cut a swathe through the venues of Manchester over the last few years, there is clearly a great deal going on for The 1975 here at the Arena; Healy had his first ever indoor cigarette here… and got away with it. He would later tell the audience that night that he had 'got off' with a girl in Year Eight here too. There's more – the venue is a matter of yards away from the site of the Urbis centre, where a young Matthew Healy would hang out on his mosher days'; it's also barely a mile across the city centre from Sound Control, where the band played to 150 people, almost exactly four years earlier. To go way back, the Manchester Arena is just 13 miles from Petit Delice, the Wilmslow cafe where Drive Like I Do hatched their initial, grand plans. Now, as the lights dimmed in the venue, those plans had become real.

'Manchester,' Healy told the crowd, after the illumination of a single pink square had kicked the crowd off into a deafening wall of screams. 'Dreams really do come true.'

But, as the gig begins and pink neon morphs into black and white cityscape backgrounds, things aren't quite right. The cavernous venue is swallowing up the initial songs – 'Love Me' and 'URGH!' – and the sound is richocheting around the site, drowning out Healy's vocals as it returns from the back wall.

It isn't until their third song, 'Heart Out' that things click together. The Madonnaesque bass-throb intro pushes deep into the arena and when George Daniel's drums lock onto it, The 1975 find their feet and are truly up and running. Healy is *laughing* during the song – at how great it sounds, at the joy of the crowd… maybe at the *ridiculousness* of the whole idea of playing an arena in their 'home' town. When the song is done he toasts the crowd with a glass of red – but only takes the merest of sips. 'Welcome to the show everybody,' he tells the crowd, his accent firmly back on its Cheshire setting. 'This is the biggest thing that we've ever done. We want to do a set that takes you through the history of The 1975 and the reasons that we are here today. So we're going deep.'

Daringly, The 1975 pull out songs like 'Milk', 'Undo' and the ambient title track of their second album, rather than guaranteed stadium-pleasers like 'The City'. This clearly isn't going to be a just a greatest hits package. 'Old songs about Manchester, that's what we need,' the singer tells the audience. 'You can't imagine how this feels for us. You're literally our people.'

The visuals change for every song – this is arena presentation on the very highest scale – as the band are surrounded by water, neon, fractured images of themselves and twinkling city vistas. As the songs change, so do the visuals. Healy is using the big screens and cameras at the venue to better effect than virtually any other performer. The 1975 heroes The Cure had played here a few weeks earlier and 90 per cent of the screen time was taken up by a shot of bass player Simon Gallup's shin. But Matthew Healy knows exactly how to use the technology to reach the furthest corner of the arena as his face fills the screens – he's directing the show from the stage, cajoling everyone to join in, wherever they are sitting.

Despite telling the audience, 'I'm not here to talk about

politics, I'm here to have a good time,' there's a telling '*but*' added to the statement. Matthew Healy is not the kind of person to shy away from from sharing what's on his mind, especially when he has an arena full of people hanging on his every word. 'When all this shit kicks off – Brexit, Trump – we all get very defensive,' he tells them, in an echo of his speech at Glastonbury earlier in the year. 'There's a hardening of positions on each side. The left goes more left, the right goes more right. It's sad to see so many young voices of progression being drowned out by regressive ideas. It's not just about race, gender, age. But if we are young and we are pissed off and we are compassionate and we are progressive it's our responsibility to be compassionate – not be patronising – and make sure people hear how we feel, but also make sure that we hear how other people feel.'

It would be easy to mock him, but a more sensible piece of advice at the end of 2016 would be hard to find – all from a young man with a bootlace tie, a funny haircut and a red wine stain down the front of his shirt.

After 'Paris', Girls' and 'Sex' the band leave, only to return with another off-centre, unusual choice, 'Medicine'. The track, written for the ill-fated, Zane Lowe-curated re-soundtracking of the movie *Drive* might not seem like the first choice for an arena encore, but here in Manchester, it works. In response, the audience illuminates the venue with thousands of camera-phone lights. Healy – inevitably – bursts into tears.

'This is the best city in the whole fucking world,' Healy

helpfully informs the crowd. 'Let's go mental!' The double punch of 'Chocolate' and 'The Sound' signal the end of the band's homecoming. 'Manchester, thank you for the best show we've ever played.' With that, the band leave the stage – Hann was last to exit, it was like he didn't want to leave.

On the whole, reviewers felt the band had pulled off their elevation to fully-fledged arena act: 'Straight off the back of their US tour, Matthew Healy and the rest of The 1975 returned to Manchester last night with their biggest-ever hometown show at the Arena,' said the *Manchester Evening News*. 'The Prince-esque guitar riffs of opener "Love Me" blew through the speakers as the room erupted into pure hysteria. The 1975 have fervent fans – although the show wasn't quite a sell-out. If there was still doubt in anyone's mind that these boys were the real deal though, it was gone in an instant. Healy prowled up and down the stage, playing the crowd like a seasoned frontman, rising and falling with his every move.'

Some long-term supporters within the music press felt that they – and the band – had been proved right about an act that were considered by some to be a joke: 'It feels as if a lot of people have done a bit of a U-turn on The 1975 this year,' pointed out the review of the show on *The Line of Best Fit* website. 'There's probably never been fiercer competition for the average listener's attention than there is in the current musical climate and given Healy's penchant for deliberately playing up to the image of the dickhead rock star, you can perhaps forgive detractors for hearing a couple of gaudy singles, seeing something as deliberately brash as the "Love Me" video or February's *Saturday Night Live* performance and jumping to the wrong conclusions. It's precisely because of that that the nerveless manner in which the band have navigated consistently choppy waters should be hugely commended; they've endured through years of rejection from major labels, and the changing tide of critical and public opinion. There aren't enough characters like Healy in music any more; he, like his band, exudes a potent mixture of self-obsession and self-assurance and he, like his band, feels like a bit of a one-off.'

* * *

After Manchester the tour would continue with a two-night stand at The O2 in London. Again there was a sense that many music writers had been caught out by The 1975's rise: 'This success is all the more remarkable as the The 1975's musical default mode is a strain of intelligent yet scratchy, mildly funky electropop that can recall long-forgotten mid-80s pop outliers,' offered the *Guardian*. 'Johnny Hates Jazz. Red Box. *Belouis Some*. It's an impression confirmed early in tonight's set as force-of-nature singer Matthew Healy lounge-lizards across stage in a tuxedo, a glass of red wine in hand, to sing "UGH!", about his former cocaine habit. Yet The 1975 get away with these acts of aggressive magpie archeology because they write great, sharp-edged pop songs with nagging, irresistible hooks. Combined with stellar lighting, it makes this a hugely classy state-of-the-art arena show that charms even as you play spot the influences. "Loving Someone" has trace elements of Scritti Politti's arch, sumptuous meta-pop; the thrumming synths and choked vocals of "Somebody Else" could be Tears for Fears, were they fronted by a rag doll with a messiah complex.'

Something's don't change though – one being some reviewers inability to accept the key element of the band: their free-for-all flitting from one genre to another: 'The group, along with frontman Matthew Healy, barreled through some of the finest pop funk from their latest release,' read the review in London's *Metro*. 'The swaggering Prince-inspired jams like "Love Me" and "UGH!" showcase Healy at his fascinating cocksure best; with his saunters across the stage clutching a glass of red wine possessing the kind of extravagant ridiculousness the UK pop scene is sorely lacking… It's only when the band lean heavily on the instrumentals littered throughout their albums where the show begins to wobble. Initially interesting deviations like "An Encounter" and the minimalist "Please Be Naked" devolve into toilet-break fodder in the latter half of the set, especially when awkwardlyrubbedalongsidethesoaringlikesof"She'sAmerican".

There was one person in the audience at The O2 who certainly understood, even if the reviewer from the *Metro* didn't: former Drive Like I Do guitarist Owen Davies was there on the second night. He went backstage to see his old friends after the show: 'Well, it was amazing,' Davies told me. 'I was saying to the boys afterwards that each venue gets bigger and bigger but they don't look or feel out of place – to be honest the production quality fits a venue of that size now.

And the fact they've sold out the arena tour now is incredible. I honestly wouldn't be surprised if they did Wembley in the next two years. I was talking to George about the contrast between The O2 and when we played a gig on the back of a lorry in Newcastle in front of about two old age pensioners at some weird fair day at a racecourse. Big difference!'

The difference that Davies highlights appears to be an external one – The 1975, Healy in particular, always seemed to *know* they'd be huge. Cast your mind back to the band playing free gigs at the start of 2013, with the singer acting as if he was playing an arena. Maybe he was just practising for when the day actually arrived. Though Healy may have always known it would happen, how and why it happened seems to be a piece of magic he doesn't want to think about too much, for fear of jinxing it. 'If I knew, I'd be doing it more,' he told Dork magazine in 2016. 'If there was remotely a formula to it, I'd have done it another two times. Do I have to care? Like, because I can feel like I can appreciate it without intellectualising it too much. I don't want to review it. That's the sort of thing you do when you come out of a relationship. Maybe when we break up, I'll do a mind retrospective where I'll figure everything out but right now, I'm really humble and I'm very lucky. I don't think people realise how much we do it for ourselves. Anytime you pull a leather jacket on or go out on stage, there's an element of showmanship there. What The 1975 really is, is me and George smoking weed in a bedroom and making records. That's all we do.'

THE 1975

From the earliest days playing gigs for their teenage peers for Macclesfield Youth Bands to the Manchester Arena, the level of confidence in their own abilities and possibilities never seemed in doubt. It's hard to begrudge them their success – the level of work involved is not in question. From Sound Control to the Arena in four years is no mean feat. To start their attack on the nation's arenas in Manchester, that must have been sweet.

Imagine the scene, backstage at the Manchester Arena for that first night of the tour. It would have been buzzing, awash with family and friends. Healy's parents were there along with his step-parents. The Healy's former Alderley Edge neighbour Peter Hook even showed his face – perhaps reminding Matthew about the time he'd told him he was forming a band.

Backstage after a triumphant homecoming gig for The 1975… I wonder if there were any National Lottery scratch-cards?

Probably not.

TWELVE

THIS EFFEMINATE, GOTH, EIGHTIES, R&B, ROCK 'N' ROLL, MODERN-ART THING

In an otherwise pretty positive review of The 1975's debut album, journalist Michael Hann made the following observation when it came to what he saw as some of the band's more suspect characteristics: 'It's a salutary reminder that if you time travel back to the 1980s, you risk returning with Cutting Crew spliced into your DNA.'

Hann meant it as a criticism of course – but there would have been plenty of people reading his piece who would have quietly whispered under their breaths, *God, I love Cutting Crew – '(I Just) Died in Your Arms Tonight': what a tune!* That's because the eighties that The 1975 tap into is not the eighties that tends to be populated by music critics; it's not the John Peel-centred decade of The Smiths, The Wedding Present and The Fall. It's the eighties of Go West, George Michael,

Phil Collins and Simple Minds. It's the uber-bright, in-your-face, big-haired, blokes-in-makeup era of electro pop, drum machines and chorused guitars that you won't find being celebrated in the musical history books – and that's because those books tend to be written by the same music writers who ignored it the first time around.

One band's insult is another band's glowing endorsement. Matthew Healy's former neighbour Peter Hook – of Joy Division and New Order – recently told me he thought The 1975 sounded like Hall & Oates. He meant it as a bad thing; Matthew Healy would no doubt see it as a huge compliment. 'I think the eighties has become quite naff and it's been abused in pop culture – I'm not obsessed with 1980s music,' Healy told *Stereoboard*, perhaps protesting too much. 'But I think coincidentally all of my favourite artists were at their peak [then] – Whitney Houston, Michael Jackson, Peter Gabriel – that's when they made their career-defining work.'

The eighties seems to have been hotwired into the band from the start – literally from their first ever gig; and again, it's that 'wrong' kind of eighties, the eighties that the critics don't tend to approve of. Former Drive Like I Do guitarist Owen Davies: 'Going back to those old gigs – "Ghostbusters", "Livin' On A Prayer" – we kind of always had a love for the eighties, everyone in the band did. So it doesn't surprise me that they've gone down that road – but I think it's brilliant.'

Despite just sneaking in by being born in the last year of the decade, Matthew Healy is, in many ways, a young man born in the wrong time. As a frontman, it would have been interesting to see how he would have fared up against the likes of Michael Hutchence, Prince and Pete Burns in their pomp. 'I genuinely do believe that if The 1975 had existed in the 1980s,' Healy told *Clash* magazine in that self-effacing way of his, 'we would have been one of The Great Eighties Bands.'

One of the reasons The 1975 have achieved such success is perhaps down to this conscious or unconscious referencing of the 1980s. The benefits are clear: to an older generation, it provides a set of references that they can immediately understand and relate to – in the same way that sampling a classic track can bring a new audience on board with hip-hop. To a younger audience, it can seem impossibly shiny and new, especially if couched in lyrics that speak directly to you about your life. If you can pull this trick off, you've immediately doubled your potential audience.

The 1975 are not the only act to carry out this style of musical reverse-engineering; Haim have convinced two generations that their Prince-meets-Fleetwood Mac brand of soft rock is something new. When they started to get noticed in America, The 1975 were sometimes referred to as the 'male Haim'. Washington band Brett have honed a brand of dreamy, 4am, comedown synth pop that rivals the best moments of The 1975's quieter side. UK act Years & Years have tapped into a similar vein, finding a meeting point between Yazoo and Freeez.

Selling pop music that has something to say is not easy.

The 1975 have managed it in the twenty-first century by harking back to bands who managed to walk that most tricky of tightropes in the past. Some critics may sneer and drop references to Cutting Crew and Hall & Oates, but the clearer link to the past is via a band like Scritti Politti, to my ears the act that most closely resembles The 1975. Led by the charismatic Green Gartside, Scritti's roots mirror those of The 1975. Both started out at the noisy and punky end of the market but soon developed an ear – and an eye – for a shiny and seamless pop-funk aesthetic. Look no further than Scritti's astonishing *Cupid & Psyche 85* album to hear how much they have influenced The 1975.

Healy has acknowledged they were listening to Scritti in the run-up to recording their second album: 'The reason we reference the eighties so much, it's not because of particular bands or particular songs,' he explained to MTV, 'it's because it was a time when pop music wasn't so encumbered with self-awareness and fear and cynicism. I wasn't there – "grunge killed pop" – I don't know what happened. But I know that pop music existed where [there were] records like *So* by Peter Gabriel and *Tango in the Night* by Fleetwood Mac – amazing records that could almost be considered as supermarket favourites, but also really credible, forward-thinking pieces of work.

'That doesn't really exist as much anymore. Pop music now, if it's massive in the charts, is tarnished with a lack of credibility, or a sense of that. Because, fair enough, there's a lot of shit, and people don't know what they're allowed to like. It's really difficult to see in pop music what's a genuine expression and what's just something that's a commercial statement. The thing with pop music, with me, the only question I allow myself is: Well, do you believe it?'

Another stick that has been used to beat the band with has been emo. The catch-all term has been attached to everything from underground, hardcore 'emotional' punk to platinum-selling mainstream acts and was used as a way to describe the early incarnations of The 1975. If they've carried anything forward from those days – from Me And You Versus Them via Drive Like I Do – it's an incredibly strong sense of ownership and connection with their fans. In the world of The 1975, emo – like the eighties – is nothing to be ashamed of: 'It's the new emo,' George Daniel explained to *Rolling Stone*. 'If you take the word emo at face value, where it came from emotional music, not the pop-punk crossover nonsense. It just was a pigeonhole for emotional rock music that came out at a certain time. What it means is that it was over the top and a lot of it was super-ridiculous. It addressed stuff like depression and talking about relationships. We connect with our fans in an extreme format. I don't think that's a reflection of any musical connection with that world at all. The tribalism, and the fans feel like we're theirs.'

The 1975 – and Healy in particular – could never be accused of dragging around a surplus of self-doubt. Think back to those early gigs: of Healy thanking each section of an audience at the end of a show as if he was playing Wembley, when in fact he'd just finished a free pub gig in Yorkshire. Manchester music legend Tony Wilson once described Joy Division as 'being onstage because they had no fucking choice'. The 1975 seemed to operate on a similar system: 'We can't do anything else,' Healy told *FaceCulture* around the time of their first album being released. 'It's not a question of whether it's an honest expression of who we are. It's the only expression that we have. And that's bought from being totally narrow-minded and blind. We never thought of the idea of it not happening.'

What about those involved in the band's story – what do they believe are the reasons The 1975 have broken through with something so heartfelt that's also a commercially viable entity? Why them? Why now? 'The songs are great for a start,' says Dan Deighan, who followed the band through their chameleon-like changes from Drive Like I Do to The 1975: 'They always had pop songs,' Deighan told me. 'Those songs they played at [Manchester pub] The Phoenix – how many people have heard those songs since then? Some of those songs are ten years old – they've stood the test of time already and the band aren't even thirty. It was always well-structured, well thought out and they've worked really hard for it.'

The concept of cherry-picking ideas, sounds and influence from wherever takes your fancy is one of Matthew Healy's favoured processes. He has constantly tried to position The 1975 as representatives – spokesmen might be pushing it a bit

– for their generation; a multi-platform generation accessing a grab bag of whatever takes their fancy. The *New York Post* once cannily described them as 'the ultimate millennial band': 'We're a band that defines a certain generation at a certain time,' Healy explained to the *Guardian*. 'Nobody my age consumes media in a linear, straightforward way; it's like a human eye, light coming in from everywhere. You can expect a seventeen-year-old girl to be listening to Kendrick Lamar and to Carole King. I think we're the first band to really embrace the fact there aren't many rules left.'

Dan Deighan agrees: 'I hate anyone generalising about genres of music. I like indie, so I'm not allowed to like pop? That's ridiculous. Lads go to the gigs and like The 1975, so do fourteen-year-old girls. It's not a problem.'

It certainly isn't a problem for Matthew Healy: 'Anybody of any kind of intellect understands that the most active people as consumers of music are young women,' he explained to US journalist Meaghan Garvey. 'The most active people on social media, when you come to talking about music, are young women. Mary Shelley wrote *Frankenstein* when she was eighteen, do you know what I mean? There's fans of ours that I meet that are far smarter than me. Of course they scream and they go wild – but if I was young and really, really excited, and drunk, and my favourite band was there, I'd be screaming and going wild… I'm not going to apologise for embracing this intense emotional investment that I get from people. Because it's a big deal.'

Dan Deighan again: 'They're writing really good pop songs. There's nothing wrong with pop. I'm a fan of pop. I can't stand the snobbery. As if fourteen-year-old girls aren't allowed an opinion. It's boring. And patronising.'

'We embrace being a big pop band,' Healy told *Billboard* in 2014, just after their first taste of true success with their debut album. 'Not too many "cool" bands are viewed like that, wanting to be mass appeal. As a band we're coming up to eleven years now, and having a year of everything you've ever dreamed of doesn't actually negate the rest of the time you spent as a band. It was good for us. It really allowed us to build a relationship between four people, and we never let ego take centre stage. It's a democracy, based on our relationships with each other.

'This band isn't something I do frivolously; it's not a party trick. It's who I am. Understanding those things has been the most beneficial thing about this year. If you sign to a major label when you're sixteen, you just go fucking mental, don't you? Insane. With us, because we dreamed about it for so long, we just get to go out and go on tour and let things happen to you and feel like we can handle it.'

The success of The 1975 is baffling in some ways, though – because their records can be so downright *odd*. It's unlikely that their guitar-toting contemporaries would turn in something as challenging and difficult as 'Please Be Naked'. But the unashamed pop of The 1975 – alongside their ambient noodlings and glacial post-rock instrumentals – is a tempting way to introduce listeners to the more leftfield aspects of their music – or the music of others. 'One of the things that I love about The 1975 is now I've realised that we're kind of this gateway band,' Healy explained to MTV. 'Gateway bands used to exist, but they were normally shitty – you know, bands that straddled between the truly alternative scene and the mainstream market. A soft, easy band for the kids to transition from the Backstreet Boys to fuckin' Cannibal Corpse or whatever it may be. With us, of course we're gonna get a lot of kids who were into, I don't know, 5 Seconds of Summer. And then they get inside and they realise: I can stay here. I can grow with this band. This isn't a faddy thing. This isn't the Backstreet Boys. You're not being told to like us.'

Promoter Ben Hiard certainly liked something about the five-piece Drive Like I Do on Myspace enough to make him want to put on their gigs in Manchester in 2007: 'It just seemed to click at the right time,' is his view of The 1975's success. 'The music industry was over-saturated with bands trying to sound like they were from the eighties. They came across like a modern band who just happened to have grown up listening to that kind of music. It didn't seem like they were trying to be Huey Lewis and The News or anything. It was more a case of, "This is the music that we like so we are going to use these influences."

'I play their stuff at club nights all the time. And it works. It works with people in Blink-182 T-shirts and baggy shorts, it works with girls in dresses, it works with guys in skinny jeans and leather brogues on. They really do appeal to so many people now. Why? Because they are *that* good. He [Matthew Healy] has substance and they have substance.'

For Ben Taylor, the man who put on that Sound Control gig in 2012 that proved to be such a pivotal moment for the band, The 1975 are a proposition that keep improving, on their albums and in the live arena: 'The first album was packed with singles,' he told me. 'The second record – I love it. It's a completely different monster. It's got a lot of legs. It's clever, it's well written, the production is great. It feels like a stadium band. Their light show with the 3D mapping is probably the best I've seen. They've taken it up a notch. It'll be interesting to see what comes next. A Mötley Crüe flying drum kit, maybe?'

It's inevitable perhaps that this book has been as much about Matthew Healy as about The 1975. He dominates the level of interest in the band and he commands attention in every situation. There is a telling image of the band in the May 2016 issue of Q magazine that features The 1975 on its cover. It's of Daniel, Hann and MacDonald, in a perfectly straightforward three-shot, looking at the camera. Healy is off to the right, pulling a dramatic pose as he stares at himself in a mirror with his hand touching his own reflection. The caption reads: 'Can you spot the lead singer in this band?'

Healy is the unapologetic focus of The 1975 – it's good for business and he's very good at it; he's the best frontman and the best pop star this country has produced for a very long time.

He does the talking too: 'The band don't really talk. I talk – a lot,' he once told the *Evening Standard*, perhaps unnecessarily.

In any other band, the other three members of The 1975 would be considered way above average in terms of being articulate pop stars. Any journalist who has tried to prod a few words out of an exhausted, disengaged musician will tell you that. But in The 1975, it's hard to get a word in edgeways when Matthew Healy is around. 'It's not a surprise that Chris Martin's more famous than the bass player of Coldplay,' drummer George Daniel pointed out to *SPIN* magazine. 'It doesn't bother us at all… And [Healy] needs it, he needs that element, and I think that's partly the reason that our band does so well. Because there's not really very many frontmen that aren't scared anymore.'

George Daniel – the last of the original five members of You And Me Versus Them to join the band – seems to be the one person that Healy defers to. The songs start with them – and are then expanded on and enhanced by Hann and MacDonald. But it's Daniel to whom Healy gives the most credit: 'He's a genius, he's amazing, and all of the sounds that sound like The 1975, like, *Oh that's a 1975 sound* – that's all George,' Healy told *Coup de Main* magazine in 2016. 'Me and George are a complete 50/50 composite. Sometimes I come up with more technically minded things and he'll come up with a more philosophical idea for a song, but normally, he will create something and then I will say how it makes me feel or what it makes me think about, and then musically, we'll get involved with it. I don't know what we'd do without each other. Like a lot of bands, it's kind of an autocratic situation, so we all have our own position that we live in. I think the most important thing with a band is that you need to have a dynamic where everybody respects everybody's opinion at face value. So we don't have many arguments [about songwriting], we don't have many discussions about that kind of thing.'

'He's fleetingly obsessive,' says Daniel of Healy. 'He'll turn up with a video camera and projector: "Look, I'm making a film." Yeah, all right. Two weeks later, he's lost the camera charger and he's forgotten about it. That's what makes him great when he's focusing on his work. He's either all the way on or all the way off.'

'Why are they so successful? My gut answer would be because of Matt Healy,' says journalist Emily Brinnand, who has followed the band's fortunes since 2012. 'Because of his personality – the way that he comes across. He's very aware of it. He's the man you think of when you think of The 1975… The 1975? Oh yes, Matt Healy. He's the image of that band and that's maybe the reason why they've got to where they have reached. Couple that with the sound that they originally came out with – poppy and instantly catchy – it's what's made them rocket. The other Manchester bands that were around when The 1975 came through are still kind of underground, very cool, very art house-y. And I think that's still something The 1975 want – but they have got the girls, the fan base. He's [Healy] been put on a pedestal as the sexy frontman and he will get admirers – boys and girls to follow him around. Other bands, they didn't get that because maybe they were more of a collective.'

Healy's abilities as a performer – while simultaneously being aware of the inherently ridiculous notion of what he is doing – make him the first *post*-frontman. 'I bring a self-awareness to it,' he explained to journalist Patrick Doyle. 'I'm not, like, Vanilla Ice basking in the glory with my shirt off. When we started getting bigger, and the dynamics started to present itself of the screaming girls and me, that had never happened before. But you can't stop it. So when you do something and they scream, you have to kind of buy into it, in a way. It's just about confidence. There's no leather jackets or cultural relevance or getting laid going on in my head. It's the pursuit of the form of it and it's like a real thing that's really deep within me, so I'm very lucky now because that's twinned with this kind of *amazing* appreciation. *This is what I'm supposed to be doing.* It's kind of like requested of me.'

The attention that Healy now receives is extreme – think of those suitcases full of intensively personal gifts that fans have given him as he travels the world. The verbal reactions he provokes from fans can be extreme, too: 'They say [shouting] "FUCK ME",' Healy told the *Moshcam* video channel. 'They say that to me! Can you imagine any other social situation where you could shout that at someone's face? Can you imagine being in a queue at the shops and saying to someone "FUCK ME" just like that? Can you imagine? You're not allowed to do that. You'd be amazed at the shit that gets said to my face, stuff you could only imagine. It's a weird world we live in.'

Perhaps the greatest piece of sleight of hand that Healy has achieved so far is the way he has sidestepped the notion of himself as a 'celebrity offspring'. In the eyes of the British media, this is possibly the naffest thing you could be. He's played this game extremely well – Denise Welch and Tim Healy are now probably better known in many quarters as Matthew Healy's parents, rather than the other way around. But Healy junior has always been acutely aware of this – sometimes having to subtly distance himself from his parents – especially his headline-hogging mum. When Denise Welch released her first book, *Pulling Myself Together*, in 2010, it featured a variety of pictures of her family, including plenty of Matthew Healy. In her second book, *Starting Over*, in September 2012 – just as The 1975 were breaking through – her son was notably absent from the photo section. Instead there was a photo of Healy's foot, bearing a rose tattoo accompanied by the name 'Denise'. Not 'Mum' but 'Denise'. The picture has the caption, 'The only photo I'm allowed of my son Matt!'

It appeared that the singer didn't want photos of him looking un-1975 just as he was planning to put the finished version of his band out there. Healy has become a success in music despite, not because of, his parents: 'Coming up in a rock 'n' roll band, aspiring to credibility, and having parents that are part of this, at times, ITV [world] – it's hard to be cool and do what I do,' he admitted to *The Independent*. 'Because people just assume nepotism – "he's a celebrity kid" – I have never, ever utilised [it]. I mean, what connection does somebody who's in *Coronation Street* and a guy who used to be in *Auf Wiedersehen, Pet* have in the rock 'n' roll world? People go, Oh, he's had it easy… I've had it harder!'

In the earliest press stories about The 1975, there was no mention of his famous parents. Healy seemed to take a perfectly sensible 'don't ask, don't tell' approach if the journalist in question didn't know about his background – but he wasn't about to pretend he was someone that he wasn't either. 'I suppose in the early days I had to tread carefully and what I didn't want to do was ostracise myself by denying it,' he told US journalist Joe Leary. 'In America, people's mindset is different. Over here you get people like Justin Timberlake or JLo, where American culture has a kind of a good view, actually, and you can do whatever you want. If you want to be an actor you can be just as credible an actor as a singer. In the UK it doesn't work like that and you stick to what you know. There's also a fear that you're just a celebrity's kid and don't have integrity in your own right. All I did was make sure that my band was better than the other bands.'

Charlie Watts – who came across the band as Drive Like I Do as a teenager at university and went to many of The 1975's early gigs – exemplifies the kind of south Manchester/ Cheshire kid who made up their early fan base. 'They came from the Manchester music scene, but they were never like Oasis and Stone Roses – they're my age and their songs are relevant to people my age,' is his view. '"Chocolate" is about driving around in a car smoking weed and getting stopped by the police. It was relevant and it just sort of appealed to me; I think that's what The 1975 tapped into. Oasis and Stone Roses was very much about "lad" behaviour, whereas The 1975 were more about kids – teenagers – growing up, wanting to do stuff you can't do when you're under eighteen. That's what the appeal was to me.'

'The thing that I loved was the whole "We only wear black, that's our thing, we only post photos in black and white, we don't want to conform to the media…" That sort of spiel. I just thought it was cool, there was no one else out there doing it at the time. They seemed to be a band that appealed to females and males. Obviously they're not everyone's cup of tea. I can't imagine a big Oasis fan being a huge The 1975 fan. But I was someone who was like open to either sides of the spectrum and they found a niche in the market to put both sides together. I think that's why they got so big. Even my dad likes them.'

If nothing else, The 1975 have put Wilmslow on the musical map. No longer will the town be the kind of place that rock stars retire to. But the place they are most associated with didn't seem to even notice their swift ascent: 'The first time I'd heard of them was when I was interviewing Denise Welch and it was to do with a book launch here in Wilmslow,' admits Peter Devine of the *Wilmslow Guardian*. 'She said to me, "Oh my son's in this band – The 1975." I'd never heard of them! I thought she'd mispronounced the name. They'd passed me by. But it's to do with age. I never heard anyone saying, "Have you heard of this band The 1975?" She was trumpeting them. When I asked around, it was the younger members of staff who'd heard of them. They definitely took us unawares.'

In fact, a whole generation of musicians and producers has sprung up from the Wilmslow area in recent years, many of them contemporaries of Matthew Healy and his band. Former Drive Like I Do guitarist Owen Davies: 'The thing in particular with Wilmslow, you've got our friend Elliott [Williams], he plays keyboards for Editors now, he was at school with us. The band Spring King, who are emerging now, half of them went to Wilmslow High as well. Same age as us. Tarek [Musa] the singer in that band produced one of our early recordings. Some people think there's something in the water there, everybody seems to do well musically, from Wilmslow… very strange.'

Many of the band's contemporaries have come on board as well – working alongside them on everything from lighting to merchandise. Healy's often asked if he misses home; no, he replies, because many of my mates from home are with us all the time. 'I think what's important to say,' points out Owen Davies, 'is that they are fantastic at their jobs – you couldn't hand-pick someone else if you wanted to. I don't know if it's luck or what, it's just nicely worked out for everybody. I know how meticulous the guys are. If someone wasn't good enough, they'd say they're not good enough.'

From the theme to *Ghostbusters* to *I Like It When You*

Sleep For You Are So Beautiful Yet So Unaware Of It, it's been a considerable leap of faith and creativity for The 1975. The gap in ambition and the end result between their first and second albums has been huge. Expectation for what happens next is huge. 'It's always good to think that you could be like Radiohead, whereby every album is a distillation of the album that went before it,' Healy says. 'They take everything that was great from before and reinvent themselves and yet kind of do it again at the same time. It's about reinvention, but there's always a fear of alienation. Look at when Dylan went electric… I'm not comparing myself to Dylan, but I think the only way we can stay relevant is to keep reinventing ourselves. And therefore keep relevant.'

The 1975 annoy as many people as they delight – and Matthew Healy seems to take equal pleasure from both. But they seem to take the Oscar Wilde view that, 'There is only one thing in the world worse than being talked about, and that is not being talked about.'

'I'd rather people be angry and hate me rather than be bored of what they're hearing,' Healy told the Irish rock magazine *Hot Press*. 'My fear is people watching us or listening to us and not being moved at all.'

The reactions that Healy and The 1975 tend to provoke tend to be fairly extreme ones – often because people don't quite know what to make of them. They've been called 'emo funk romanticists', 'New Romantic revivalists', and 'pompous arena synth pop'. What are The 1975?